EARLY ISRAEL

EARLY ISRAEL
A New Horizon

Robert B. Coote

Fortress Press   Minneapolis

EARLY ISRAEL
A New Horizon

Cover design: Patricia Boman
Cover photo: Palphot Ltd., Israel
Internal design: Peregrine Publications

Library of Congress Cataloging-in-Publication Data

Coote, Robert B., 1944–
    Early Israel : a new horizon / Robert B. Coote.
        p.   cm.
    Includes bibliographical references and index.
    ISBN 8-8006-2450-5 (alk. paper)
    1. Jews—History—1200-953 B.C.   2. Palestine—History—To 70 A.D.
    3. Egypt—History—To 332 B.C. I. Title.
    DS121.55.C66   1990
    930'.04924—dc20   90-44950
                                                                                CIP

The paper used in this publication meets the minimum requirements of American National Standard for Information Sciences—Permanence of Paper for Printed Library Materials, ANSI Z329.48-1984.   ∞™

Manufactured in the U.S.A.   AF 1-2450
94   93   92   91   90   1   2   3   4   5   6   7   8   9   10

Contents

Preface

The purpose of this book is to summarize the understanding of early Israel that has emerged from the research of the last decade. Its emphasis rests on findings that have met more with agreement than disagreement. Within the course of the discussion I present my own views as well; some of them are novel, many of them subject to debate. But I mainly point out what are generally agreed to be important issues and relevant evidence, and where the discussion on the whole appears to be converging. The book is intended to benefit readers who are just beginning their study of early Israel, an essential topic for all students of the Bible. It does not cover the whole academic discussion, going back several decades, for which excellent summaries already exist.

Some may consider this purpose premature. But as I listen to fellow scholars who hold divergent viewpoints, and as I read their recent studies, I detect significant common ground—a growing set of shared assumptions despite important differences. In some areas I catch resolved

cadences of settled inquiry among open cadences of disagreement. Uncertainties remain: probably no two historians agree on everything. Unanswered questions still
far outnumber answered ones, and on this subject they
always will. Yet a new horizon is in view. Recent research
on early Israel has brought us to a new understanding.

A related purpose of this book is to help dispel the aura
surrounding early Israel. The origin of Israel, while indeterminate, is not, in my view, a mystery. Nor does it
provide a key for unlocking the mysteries of Jewish and
Christian faith and culture. To understand early Israel,
one must once and for all leave behind the idea of an ideal
community. One must set aside notions of the unique or
sublime ethnic, national, religious, moral, or social character of Israel, early or otherwise, and instead examine
the sparse evidence with an eye for what is usual, normal,
and expected in the history of Palestine. This perspective,
more than any particular theory about early Israel, is the
essence of the current shift in understanding, and this is
what, contrary to appearances, makes the subject important to everyone interested in the Bible.

I recently coauthored a more technical work on early
Israel with Keith Whitelam, *The Emergence of Early Israel
in Historical Perspective*.[1] It provides a detailed methodo-
logical discussion with particular attention to historical
geography. With qualifications, its conclusions remain
basic to my thinking. However, there is little overlap
between that book and the present one. Readers familiar
with the earlier book will immediately recognize differences, particularly with respect to the political emphasis
of this book. Not even the concise version of Israel's origin
presented here is to be found in the earlier book. This
book is a history, not a discussion of method.

The present work represents an expansion of the historical sketch in chapters 5 and 6 of *The Bible's First History,* by David Ord and myself,[2] and brings the story to

the point where my book on the Elohist's history (forthcoming from Fortress Press), chapter 5, picks it up, namely with David's death. Together these three books treat the history of Israel from its beginning to its revolt against the house of David. The treatment of J in chapter 7 of this book takes *The Bible's First History* as its point of departure.

I have intentionally kept notes to a minimum. Resources and named references relating to each chapter can be located easily in the bibliography.

The subject matter of this book continues under active investigation. This work took its present shape only recently, after a decade and a half of learning in the same classroom with Marvin Chaney. Those familiar with his research will recognize his influence here in several places. It is a privilege and pleasure to work with someone who finds it quite acceptable to see eye-to-eye on the questions though not on all the answers, and I acknowledge my debt to him.

Introduction

This book attempts to explain in concise terms what ancient Israel was in the beginning and how it came to be. To do so it is necessary to dispel the mystique attached to this subject. Israel's emergence in the annals of human history is not significant by virtue of uniqueness. Rather, the process involved political relations more or less typical of Palestine. This was Albrecht Alt's premise when he initiated the critical analysis of early Israel some seventy years ago, and it remains valid today.[1] Early Israel was a typical, changeable political organization with ruling sheikhs, clients, and laboring constituents entangled in and compromised by power and fear no less than other similar groups, not an unprecedented national, ethnic, social, or religious entity with an unparalleled and persistent essence. Protest raised by Gottwald against such essentialist categorizations forms the bedrock of all future understanding of early Israel.[2]

The current revolution in the understanding of early Israel is of importance to everyone interested in the Bible. How did Israel originate? It is now clear that there was

1

no conquest of highland Palestine by outside invaders as told in the Bible, no infiltration of disparate nomads into the Palestine hills to merge gradually in a tribal league as proposed by Alt and Noth, and no peasant revolution as proposed by Mendenhall and Gottwald.[3] These views as such no longer apply, although ingredients of all three rightly continue to play an important role in the understanding of early Israel. This book focuses not on the debate among and about these views, which is well presented in many sources, but on what, as a result of various findings and stimuli, is emerging in their place. What we need is not some fourth compelling alternative, but rather a change in what we understand the search for the origin of Israel to be about. Thus this book is less a summary of current scholarship, to which it is indebted, and more an indication of where current scholarship leads.

Readers might well wonder whether an entire book, even a short one, is needed to dispel an assumption as improbable as that of a unique entity with a unique genesis about which there are virtually no historical records. Yet a whole shelf of books, including the recent landmark works by Gottwald, Chaney, Halpern, Lemche, and Finkelstein, might fail to quash such an assumption, so instinctive is the notion of Israel's unprecedented cohesion and rectitude, both because of and despite the doctrines of the Hebrew Scriptures. The Hebrew Scriptures were not written in early Israel; neither their unique message nor their genius originated there, even though one basic trait of the Scriptures, their ambiguous stance toward the temple state, can be traced to early Israel. The writers of the Hebrew Scriptures knew little or nothing about the origin of Israel, although the Scriptures can provide much information relevant to the investigation of early Israel. The period under discussion, therefore, does not include the periods of the patriarchs, exodus, conquest, or judges, as devised by the writers of the Scriptures. These periods never existed. As scriptural historians increasingly recognize, the continued use of such periods in histories of the scriptural period constitutes a grave disservice.

I hardly expect readers to welcome the demise of the notion of Israel's golden age without a satisfactory replacement. That, however, is difficult to provide where so little is known. The most satisfying history is narrative history. Unfortunately, the scriptural narrative is the only narrative source for early Israel so far. Since the scriptural narrative, however, has little to do with early Israel, there can be no narrative history of early Israel. Such a narrative would certainly be welcome, and in this regard future generations may be more fortunate than ourselves. Who knows what riches of history lie buried in the great portion of the Middle East and Palestine that to date remains unexcavated?

This book focuses mainly on the final century of the Egyptian New Kingdom in Palestine, the century and a half of Philistine dominance in lowland Palestine, and the formation of the Israelite and Judahite monarchies in highland Palestine. In addition, again as with Alt but for a different purpose, considerable attention is given to the background and nature of Egyptian imperialism in Palestine. The historical end leaves of my treatment of Israel are set by the only reference to early Israel outside the Hebrew Scriptures, from the court of Pharaoh Merneptah of Egypt, ca. 1207 B.C.E.,[4] and by references to Israel in documents from the court of David preserved in the Scriptures, written not long after 1000 B.C.E.

The problem posed by these end points is this: What was the nature of the Israel referred to by Merneptah, and how did that Israel develop into David's Israel? Although this period comprises over two hundred years—no less than the entire history of the United States—what is known about it as pertains to Israel remains exceedingly schematic. As Lemche observes, the primary datum is our ignorance.[5] A short book on the origin of Israel will weigh less than a long one, but may be more in keeping with what little is known.

The origin of Israel need not be a complicated subject, at least as far as the basics go. It proceeds from two archaeological givens. The first is a reference to Israel from the fifth year of Merneptah, an inscription (with possibly a pictorial representation) that identifies Israel as a military force in Palestine and indicates that in the last decade of the thirteenth century B.C.E. it was neither a city nor a state. The second is evidence of the spread of villages on the settlement frontiers of Palestine during the twelfth and eleventh centuries B.C.E. These new settlements housed much of the population called Israel in early scriptural texts and ruled by a king of Israel by the end of the eleventh century.

These two givens, the Merneptah *stela* and the spread of settlement, have been known for a long time. What then is new, and what changes our thinking about early Israel? The revolution in our understanding is based on the recent wealth of new archaeological data and on new perspectives from archaeology, comparative ethnography, historical geography, and classical literary analysis. All these put what has been known in a different light.

The new horizon referred to in the subtitle has eight aspects (which at least hint at the outline of a sparse narrative):

1. *Israelites were indigenous to Palestine.* Most were poor farmers and farm workers and their families. The main political influence over their lives was the *struggle of hierarchical factions linked to outside powers.*

2. *Egyptian imperial power* dominated Palestine from the late sixteenth century B.C.E. and *peaked in the thirteenth and early twelfth centuries.*

3. *During the first three centuries of Egyptian power in Palestine,* economic and political exploitation disrupted social relations and aggravated intraregional hostilities. As a result, *settlement retreated* from frontier zones and *population declined.*

4. In 1207 B.C.E. *Israel was a strong tribal confederacy developed by Egypt and Palestinian chiefs* to oversee tribal interests and the border zone between the Egyptian and Hittite spheres of interest. Its one-time chief Moses was an Egyptian agent. Its constituents primarily inhabited the lowlands of northern Palestine, as both villagers and tent dwellers. The notion of a uniform Israel applied only to the variable elite political organization of the tribes of Israel as conceived by Egyptian and native masters and their closest constituency.

5. *European and western Anatolian invaders overran lowland Palestine during the last century of the Egyptian empire.* In 1200–1150 B.C.E. *their strongest families took over* many areas and replaced Egyptians and Palestinians *as a ruling class.* The collapse of Egypt left this new alien elite in control of the lowlands.

6. *The collapse of the Hittite and Egyptian empires and the rise of European and Anatolian strongmen triggered an expansion of settlement and population in tribal frontier zones* in Palestine, particularly those *controlled by the tribal confederacy Israel* in part created by Egypt. Politics drove settlement. This expansion continued throughout the period of European dominance, approximately 1150-1000 B.C.E. *The population of these new settlements enlarged the tribes of Israel, whose chiefs were increasingly regarded by western Palestinians as the legitimate alternative to European and Anatolian rule.*

7. Israelite tribal society came under the monarchy of Saul in the decade around 1000 B.C.E. The incipient Israelite state was usurped by an upstart southern Palestinian

warlord, David, with the essential aid of European court followers, mercenaries, and economic organization. David extended Israelite power into the lowlands to create the only ancient state of Israel covering greater Palestine, dependent on a combination of European and Palestinian forces. *The Hebrew Scriptures began to be formed in the court of David,* where for the first time among Israelites the Europeans and Anatolians were treated as friends, and Egypt as an implacable enemy. *The earliest documents in the Scriptures contain significant hints of conditions and developments before 1000, but no historical account of Israel's origin and early history.*

8. *There was no golden age of Israel.* Israel originated wholly within the framework of recurrent political dynamics in Palestine. Early Israel constituted a typical complex tribal conglomerate in a Palestinian context ruled by a tribal elite. It embodied no ideal traits.

Each of the eight chapters in this book is devoted to one of these points. Some uncertainty surrounds each. Points 4 and 6—the nature of Israel before the settlement of the highland and the reasons for that settlement—are particularly controversial. Thus the contribution of this book to the continuing discussion is found mainly in chapters 4 through 6. This book treats topics basically in chronological order, thus preserving at least one historiographical convention. Readers should have at hand maps of scriptural Palestine, preferably showing recent archaeological sites, such as those found in the *Oxford Bible Atlas* or *The Harper Atlas of the Bible.*[6]

This book attempts to present only the elements of its subject. Readers who desire more will find many worthwhile studies, including those mentioned above, listed in the bibliography. No author yet can be in a position to claim knowledge of exactly how Israel originated. This applies as well to the previous book by Keith Whitelam and myself, which does however lay the groundwork for the present work. All studies since Gottwald's epochal *The Tribes of Yahweh* emphasize the preliminary nature of their investigation—as well we might, if for no other reason than the megabank of archaeological data remaining to be unearthed and interpreted. We have arrived at only the first horizon of an understanding of early Israel, which will take many years to explore. Enough is known, however, to present the basics of this revolution to readers who want to know more about it and are content to begin with a short book.

CHAPTER ONE

Making and Taking

A concept of the peoples of Palestine among whom and from whom early Israel came into being can be created with evidence from the Scriptures, other ancient texts, archaeological finds, sociological and ethnographic parallels, and descriptions of more recent times in Palestine. As with every such concept, some details are based on supposition, while the basic contours emerge from the comparative evidence.[1]

FOOD, CLOTHING, SHELTER

The peoples of ancient Palestine varied widely in their conditions and pursuits, and the Palestinians who first identified themselves as Israelites exemplified nearly the entire range. However, every one of them ate bread. There was thus one pursuit on the land on which everyone was equally dependent: the production of grains, and to a lesser extent of pulses, by rain agriculture (as distinguished from irrigation agriculture).

9

Whatever their various roles, nearly everyone played a part in this production, and everyone engaged in the struggle to keep or take as large a share as possible of the annual grain pile. As a rule, if one worked on the land, one's share was small; if one did not work, one's share was often large. The struggle for a share of food brought the residents of palace, town, village, homestead, tent, and cave together in the struggle against weather, birds, insects, and human predators, and in political and social interaction rooted in violence, which all abhorred and none evaded. The access to land and the storage, hoarding, taxing, theft, extortion, and transport of grain underlay and overrode every other concern—even its production and preparation—and bound every child, woman, and man to every other in the complex severity of Palestinian life.

The peoples of ancient Palestine made bread from hard wheat, barley, emmer, and einkorn. These grains were also eaten raw, roasted, as porridge, or brewed into beer. Wheat grew best in the broad arable of the coastal plain and alluvial lowland and highland valleys. Barley was a short-season crop more tolerant of alkaline and saline soils. It could thus be grown in places with shorter growing seasons or less rain, the hills and dry lands of Palestine.

Besides bread, the main staple was olive oil. The olive tree was suited for cultivation in most parts of Palestine, but especially in the foothills and highland. As a fat, olive oil was the best source of energy in the diet. Oil made bread and grains more palatable, and it furnished nutrients not available in grains. Oil was combined with other foods as well, for example with bread or in a hummus-like dish with pulses. Olives were not eaten whole in Palestine until the Hellenistic or Roman periods. Olive oil was also used as an ointment and as fuel for lighting.

Other foods included broad beans, lentils, chickpeas, peas, and, for the poor, vetch, all sources of vegetable protein and important for enriching the soil with nitrogen; fruits, especially grapes (also used to make wine and raisins), figs, dates, pomegranates, and apricots; nuts, including almonds, pistachios, and walnuts; milk, cheeses, curds, and yogurts; honey; carob; and edible wild plants.

For the vast majority, meat was rare. It was usually lamb. Goat, antelope and other game, pigeon, and quail meat were also eaten to some extent, pork and beef less often. Many ate meat only a few times a year, if that.

With the exception of meat, all these foods kept well. Meat could be preserved with salt, but the extent of this practice is not known. Most foods, however, were available only part of the time, when at all. Dietary variations were played on the theme of bread and oil. With little exception, when the early Israelites sat down to eat, they ate bread and oil, or just bread. Food meant bread, and the same Semitic word was used for both.

Women prepared the food. They drew water, gathered firewood, ground grain, and baked bread. They watched over the stores of grain, oil, beans, and fruit in the house or tent. At mealtime, men had first choice of helpings. Women and children ate what was left.

Most women of childbearing age were married, and of these most were pregnant or nursing. Births were spaced through weaning, which could be put off to as late as the third or fourth year. Working families were usually not large. If a woman did not die in childbirth or of some other cause during her childbearing years, she might bear as many as five to eight children, of which a fraction might survive beyond childhood. Often no children survived.

The entire family worked to produce food. Ground preparation required clearing stones and maintaining boundary dikes and stone heaps. In many places in the hills, terraces required upkeep. Men plowed the ground with a scratch plow and sowed wheat, barley, and flax in November and December. In January and February peas, chickpeas, and vegetables were put in. March found men, women, and children hoeing the weeds and grasses growing in both cultivated and fallow plots. These were saved for hay. In April the family harvested their barley and vetch, in May their wheat, peas, and lentils, in June their chickpeas. The harvested grain was borne to the village (used in this chapter to refer to the home of all workers, though not all lived in villages) threshing floor, where the stalks were beaten with a simple stick, trod upon by livestock, or smashed up with an animal-drawn sledge or wheel-thresher. The threshed material was then winnowed. The winnower tossed the material into the air for the wind to separate the grain from the straw and chaff. Meanwhile women and children used both wind and wooden shovel to clean the grain of straw and heavy particles and collect it into the family's heap. Then the grain was sieved. A quarter acre produced about a hundred pounds of wheat. When the harvest was over, the lord's agent took his share, often well over half, and the family bore the rest home in sacks or jars for storage in grain pits, silos, or bins. Before grinding or roasting the grain or crushing it for porridge, the women laboriously picked through it one more time to remove bits of grit and other impurities.

To prepare a new vineyard or restore a used one, the farmer uprooted unwanted weeds and shrubs from a plot, cleared it of surface stones, and constructed a hedge of thorn bushes or stones and a watchtower or gazebo. The vines either trailed on the ground or climbed on poles or trellises. The ground between the vines was periodically cultivated, and could be planted with annuals. The grapes began to ripen in June and were harvested from July to September. Fresh grapes could be consumed as daily fare all during August, September, and October. Between grape harvest and plowing, the vines had to be pruned, grapes dried or pressed, and, in some households, wine made.

A first crop of figs ripened in June. These were eaten fresh. In the few areas where flax was grown, it was harvested in July. Pomegranates and a second crop of figs ripened in August and September. The figs were dried and stored for the winter. Olives ripened in September, October, and November. As soon as the olives had been harvested and pressed, it was time, following the first fall rain, to plow again.

Village livestock consisted mostly of sheep and goats. Sheep and goats could be milked for up to a third of the year and the milk turned into cheese, curds, or yogurt. For most villagers, sheep and goats served as insurance more than as a regular source of food. The abundance of milk came shortly before the first grain harvest, when food supplies were at their lowest, from ewes and nanny goats nursing expendable male lambs. If the flock was at winter grazing or there were too few expendable animals, milk itself would be in short supply. In any case, milk was no long-term, consistent substitute for substantial food. Some families kept an ass, ox, or cow. Cattle were required for plowing and threshing, asses for transport. Those without an ox or cow hired from those with. The small village flocks were tended mostly by children at or near home. A larger flock in a stronger village might be led by an older youth to seasonal grazing or a customary shieling, in arid areas during the rainy winter to feed on new growth, and in cultivated areas, usually close by the village, in spring and summer to feed on field stubble and fallow growth and in the process to manure the fields.

The people wore clothing made from wool and goat hair. Thus grasses were the basis of food and clothing alike. The basic food was made from the seed of grasses palatable to humans, while the basic material for clothing was made from the hair of animals that ate less palatable grasses. Before the invention of sheep shears in the eleventh or tenth century B.C.E., wool was gathered by plucking sheep during their molting season by hand or with a bronze comb. Once shears came into use, sheep were bred for continuous growth and sheared twice a year, in the spring following lambing and in the fall. Where possible sheep were washed in a pool prior to plucking or shearing. The wool itself could make up as little as half the weight of a new fleece. The rest consisted of grease, burs, twigs, seeds, body salts, and dirt. After washing, while one man held the uncooperative beast, another would pluck or shear it. Then women took the fleece, washed it a second time, and either felted it or carded, spun, weaved, and fulled it. (Later in the scriptural period, some was dyed.) Goat hair was also collected and woven. Leather was available for clothing but was not favored. It was used for belts, straps, and sandals for men. Women and children went barefoot. Finer garments were made from linen, where available.

The production of food and clothing required numerous wooden, metal, ceramic, leather, and stone tools and utensils, such as plows, plow tips, threshing forks, pruning forks, hoes, axes, pickaxes, scrapers, yokes, harnesses, baskets, brooms, water bags, pots, storage jars, bowls, lamps, mills, and presses. These were often manufactured in the village itself by women and men with the requisite skills, or else in villages that specialized in the manufacture of a particular item.

Then as now, it rained and snowed in Palestine in the winter, and from fall until spring and at night the year round it could get extremely cold. The people of Palestine built houses to shelter themselves and their livestock. Building materials included sticks and branches, mud, mud bricks, thatch and straw, limestone, the occasional wood beam, and, rarely, lime mortar, all depending on locality and wealth. These had to be gathered and prepared for building. The floor or precinct might contain an excavated cistern or silo. Many house plans were used. Some houses consisted of rooms clustered about a courtyard. Others had more than one story, or at least a raised platform in the main room for family's living quarters. Still others were mere mud or mud-brick huts. Animals were quartered in the courtyard and on the ground floor of the house. On the main living level was found the fire, as well as storage jars, clay bins, utensils, rolled matting, and tools. There was no furniture. People slept in their everyday clothing on skins, fleeces, or plant matting, which were stored during waking hours. Livestock nearby or below provided scant warmth to dispel the nighttime chill and the damp cold of winter, with its rain and snow. In the hot months, where possible, a family managed to have a vine or fig, pine, cypress, or oak tree near their dwelling, for shade and comfort.

The people lived mostly in homesteads, villages, and towns, assemblages of anywhere from a few to a hundred or more family dwellings. Sites were selected for security and the availability of water. Houses crowded close together. Paths among the houses were narrow, crooked, and constantly changing gradient and level. Villages were typically unwalled, but could be constructed so that the outer houses formed a partial perimeter wall. Several families in the village shared a clay oven, usually a domed pit, in a nook or stone hut.

Not all lived in houses. Many destitute, insane, antisocial, or outlawed people lived in shanties or caves. It

was perfectly normal for members of tribes to live in
houses, but those—tribal or not—whose livelihood primarily involved flocks or herds and who therefore moved
from place to place within a given territory or along a
given path often lived for extended periods in tents made
of wool or goat-hair cloth draped over a wooden frame.
Nontribal villagers also on occasion resided in tents, as
when they guarded their ripening vineyards.

Most Palestinians were poor and undernourished, living at or below the level of subsistence, surrounded with
dirt, animal excrement, fleas, lice, mosquitoes, and other
insects. Work was hard, food dear, water scarce, famine
and drought a constant threat. Rain was unpredictable.
On average every third year brought inadequate rainfall;
often drought years arrived back to back. Pests, blight,
and mildew were ubiquitous. Rats, mice, birds, and insects ate more of the food than the people did. Moreover,
political forces largely beyond the working family's control intruded upon the productive regime, thus keeping
the family on subsistence fare at the mercy of erratic
circumstances, and compelling them to adopt short-term
goals with catastrophic long-term effects.

The hardships of village life left the people susceptible
to the spoliations of disease and violence. More infants
and children died than survived. Girls were especially
vulnerable, since parents favored boys. Persons who grew
to adulthood did not normally reach their genetic potential. Villagers were often stunted in their physical and
mental development. Diseases included environmental af-
flictions such as malaria, illnesses caused by unsanitary
conditions such as dysentery, trachoma, typhus, hook-
worm, and cholera, malnutrition and its repercussions,
venereal disease, rabies, leprosy, and alcoholism. Not all
of these were fatal, and not all limited to the village.
Contagions were more potent in the crowded conditions

of towns and cities. As a rule, however, the debilitations of poverty made life short and hard for the working people of Palestine. Joys there were, and glad songs and dances celebrated weddings, harvest, recovery, and vindication. The village bard sang the people's stories, the women about victory, requital, and pride. The undertone of this period, however, was the exploitation, exhaustion, fevers, rashes, itches, toothaches, fractures, mutilations, pains and hazards of childbirth, and other miseries of pre-industrial village life, and the most common songs in people's hearts were the lament and complaint.

LAND TENURE AND USE

The basic resource was land. Work on village and non-village land took many forms, all in relation to the form of land tenure that applied to the land being worked. Land tenure referred not to simple ownership but to the terms governing the use of land. These consisted of the rights, duties, privileges, and exemptions that governed residence on, occupation of, labor on, usufruct of, and claims to the product of land. Such rights were typically held by many persons at once for a given unit of land, and they changed over time. The terms of land tenure were thus multiple, multilayered, overlapping, relative, and variable. Land tenure was not a legal or social isolate; it was related to the equally fundamental and complex laws, customs, and constraints governing labor, credit and debt, kinship, patronage, mobility of persons, and distribution of wealth—in short, the systems of power and privilege that prevailed in ancient Palestine and are assumed, alluded to, and referred to throughout the Hebrew Scriptures.

The forms of work were many. Depending on a person's land rights, he or she could be a cultivating small owner; a cultivator paying a fixed rent in cash or kind; a cultivating head of a work team; a sharecropper possessing some productive helps, perhaps an ox or an ass, but not the head of a team; a sharecropper with only labor to sell, but with a regular position on a team or attachment to a parcel of land; a worker with a supposedly regular wage, paid in cash or kind; a part-time worker, perhaps hired by the day only at peak seasons; an indentured servant or debt slave; a slave at forced labor (*corvée*, or statute labor); or a slave outright. Work in the field was only one kind of work. The village could have its own shepherds, woodworkers, potters, and even metalworkers. Only part of a woman's work was in the field. Girls in poor families could be forced into slavery and prostitution, with the benefit going to the family as long as she remained a member of one.

Workers rarely if ever owned land outright as they do in modern times. They only used it and were liable to the variable exactions of kings, lords, masters, chiefs, patrons, creditors, and other claimants for extracting the produce of the land and defining its heritability. The primary claim was taxation. Taxes were collected in kind, labor, and coin. The most common was in kind. The landowner or state took as much as a half or more of the harvest. One Egyptian text from the time of early Israel describes the ordeal as follows:

> The scribe [arrives]. He surveys the harvest. Attendants are behind him with staffs, Nubians with clubs. One says to him, "Give grain." "There is none." He is beaten savagely. He is bound, thrown in the well, submerged head down. His wife is bound in his presence. His children are in fetters. His neighbors abandon them and flee. When it's over, there's no grain [left for the poor man and his family].[2]

The tax on labor (*corvée*) required a family to provide the landowner, lord, or state with workers, which could be men, women, or children, depending on the work, for a specified period of time. Work done by conscripted labor included cultivating and harvesting the lands and constructing the monumental edifices of lords and state, edifices such as temples, palaces, city walls, and earthworks. Taxes in coin could be collected where and when the rural economy was commercialized, as it often was later in the biblical period.

Different claims attached to different kinds of land. Land planted in annuals was typically more heritable than land planted in perennials, since lords and masters, the beneficiaries of tribute or trade in agricultural commodities, had an interest in encouraging the conversion of arable and mixed farming plots to commodity-producing perennials. Laws decreasing the heritability of vineyards and orchards increased the relative heritability of arable. The villager forced to put up land to secure a loan offered arable, and thus on foreclosure ended up with reduced holdings, or none at all, of the type of land that produced the family's basic foodstuff, grain for bread. All in all, those who knew how to produce food had no incentive to produce beyond subsistence, and those who had the incentive to produce as much as possible knew nothing about how it was done. This stalemate retarded the development of agricultural technology for millennia.

Villagers had reason to band together as a unit in the face of pressures from the world beyond. The village was a parochial and hostile world, regarded as sufficient unto itself though it was not, and leery of outsiders. A given custom might be practiced by as few as a single village. The culture of production varied, often considerably, from village to village, since, given the geographic diversity of Palestine, the ecological niche occupied by one village could differ considerably from that of another.

Diet, clothing, and language differed in subtle but significant ways. People could not disguise their rural origin, even the particular area or village they were from. The single village was one of scores of laterally insulated communities of food producers, dominated by overlying strata of military, administrative, and clerical lords and drones.

One way village solidarity found expression was in the communal sharing of rights to cultivate village arable. The total arable belonging to the village was periodically redistributed, or repartitioned, by lot among those families from the village, or if necessary from outside, that held cultivation rights. This practice, widespread in agrarian societies, made it easier to fallow the half or third of village arable left uncultivated each year as a single block. The village bounded the fallow block for grazing, thus preventing animals from roaming in the patchwork of cultivated and fallow plots, which would result if the land were not redistributed. Each year a different section of arable was cultivated by all the cultivating families in the village. As the arable to be planted rotated from section to section, it was redistributed. Redistribution had the additional effect of spreading the advantage of growing crops on the better village lands among the families at random. It also meant that the village paid its taxes on arable as a commonality rather than as individuals, a device that afforded some leverage against the tax collector. The lord also found this procedure the lesser evil when, as was usually the case, he lacked the bureaucratic and military capacity to tax individuals.

SOCIOPOLITICAL HIERARCHIES

The pressures disrupting worker solidarity were also strong. Primary social relations on an equal social plane extended little beyond the extended family or clan (itself dominated by adult men), in which blood feud and debt redemption were pursued with most determination. Beyond the extended family, ties of kinship and proximity were crosscut by loyalties to more powerful men whose favor was required for survival in a world in which the inevitable intercourse with the outside world was governed by favoritism. These strongmen included village sheikhs or headmen, who supposedly represented the village to the outside world and through whom the village collective paid their taxes, area masters, extortionists, estate owners, local lords, and monarchs. These were all men who could, to varying degrees, provide assistance to a villager in time of hardship, stand for a villager's rights against other chiefs and lords, represent a villager's case in legal disputation, defend the villager's interests in the endless conflicts over scarce resources that marked the villager's life, and even make it possible for the villager simply to travel beyond his or her own village, a hazard in the absence of the protection of someone with influence beyond the village. The villager was a dependent client in a world run by patrons. Access to goods, services, and opportunities depended on the friendship and personal favor of local strongmen, who related in the same way to men stronger still, and so on up the scale of power and privilege to the echelon where the two or three most powerful men, backed by their factions, were left perpetually scrambling for political supremacy.

Custom obligated a villager to help her or his friends and neighbors, and them to do likewise. A patron's obligations were less firm. His (rarely her) favor had to be cultivated, through loyalty to his cause in his own struggle for influence and power. Brokers mediated between client and patron. Brokers did not control the resources a patron did, but could facilitate contact with or access to patrons.

Many of the wealthier villagers themselves played this role, though it was usually played by noncultivators from outside the village.

The most important area in which the broker played a role was the management of credit and debt. Living at subsistence or below was precarious at best. Poverty precluded long-range planning. The vicissitudes of weather and politics often left households or whole villages destitute, with no money and little or no food or seed. In these straits the villager was forced to borrow. Rates of interest were as much as fifty or a hundred percent a year. For collateral the villager could put up an animal, his arable use rights, his labor, or the labor of another member of the family. More often than not the villager was unable to repay the debt or was mercilessly foreclosed upon. In such a case the animal or land became the patron's, or the villager or family member became a debt slave. Debt slavery was customarily limited in theory to a prescribed period, such as seven years. Even so, the slavery of a householder devastated his household. Without a claim on land and with work owed almost entirely to another, there was little chance for a family to recover economically.

Villagers demonstrated their loyalty to a patron not only by turning over land and labor to him by contract, but by supporting him in his quarrels and clashes with rivals. Life was afflicted by endemic gang warfare, fostered by patrons, whose wars they were, and sanctioned by brokers. Village factionalism was complex. Rival cleavages sliced through geographical regions, dialect divisions, tribes, clans, villages, and even families—themselves groupings that rose and fell in heroic and desperate attempts to sustain social order. The terms used to describe factional hierarchies included terms of kinship, group, and rank. The dominant factional rivalry among elites and their clients culminated by definition in the struggle for control of the state, the military and administrative organization that claimed the ultimate tenure of land. The highest title of state was king, even though kings usually could not in fact maintain uniform tenurial autonomy.[3]

Villagers resisted the encroachments of patrons and enemies in every way they could. They concealed produce. They hid themselves in hills, forests, and caves. They cheated outsiders when they could get away with it without jeopardizing their protection. They applied themselves as little as possible when forced to work. They abandoned field and village, as individuals, households, or whole villages, fleeing to a neighboring territory or resorting to banditry or some degree of nomadism in less controlled areas. Such everyday forms of peasant resistance evidenced the villagers' scorn for the prerogatives of the elite rather than the acceptance of them as inevitable, even when the villagers were forced to acquiesce. Given the right conditions, villagers could rebel in mass, although concerted worker action beyond the village was hard to achieve and impossible to sustain. Peasant revolts were common in ancient rural Palestine. Sometimes they had significant political effect on the struggle among elites, but they had no lasting effect on the general condition of workers.

Normally a second arena of tenurial autonomy and internal rivalry existed over against the state arena, an alternative set of pyramids of power and privilege within the same Palestinian society. This arena used the terminology of tribal organization, which defined relations of putative, or fictional, kinship in segmentary lineage. Often tribal organization determined land tenure in lands that the state could not control or chose to turn over to the administration of the tribe. The tribal chiefs became the taxing lords of tribally controlled arable. Sometimes, but by no means always, tribes specialized in raising sheep and goats and thus were perhaps not tied to a particular arable. The mobility of these groups contributed to their discrete social and political identity. Tribes and tribal alliances claimed autonomy and the privilege to prescind from the struggle among factions or to pursue that struggle by opposing state interference in tribal affairs. The rhetoric of autonomy rarely matched reality, as even affiliated tribes fought among themselves and, supported by matching hierarchies of clients, in the same battles as the rivals for supremacy in the state. The language of tribalism, however, indicated political claims, and often a constellation of real power over against the state, even when a tribe's main function was to provide mercenaries for the state. There were no fixed social boundaries in Palestinian society: sometimes the tribal elite themselves became the state elite. More will be said about tribal organization in chapter 4.

Palestinians did not think of themselves as belonging to any nation as that term is usually understood. The concept of a political consensus prevailing in a given territory, when it did develop, was a presumption projected by the royal court, one of the ways a king and his clerisy could attempt to override opposition and dissent and appeal to villagers as a group to counter both competing local nobles and foreign kings. As one lord among many, the king was rarely in a position to patronize the village population as a whole, though he often pretended to. Since the king was lord of a continuously expanding and contracting territory, often to extremes, the national idea always either overreached or, more often, fell short of the bounds of any distinct Palestinian culture. Everything went against defining the political unit in terms of cultural boundaries. The idea of nation, whether of Egypt, Israel, or any other, constituted a fear-mongering mystification of class and faction. Like every aspect of elite behavior, the purpose of the idea of nation in the agrarian era was to maximize the intake of grain taxes.

The ethnic purity of any supposed nation was a similar fiction. The elite of Palestine came from diverse regional, ethnic, and linguistic backgrounds. Given the vicissitudes of elite households and their sexual privileges and opportunities, genetic and cultural variety among rulers found a mirroring variety, if not so great, among the ruled. In the early centuries of the biblical period, lords in Palestine came from not only Palestine, but Syria, Egypt, Anatolia, and coastal lands covering most of the eastern Mediterranean. In later times the picture was the same. While during the entire scriptural period the indigenous village population of Palestine spoke dialects of only two languages, first the related indigenous dialects of Palestine, including Hebrew, and then dialects of Aramaic, the urban landholding population included speakers of at one time or another twenty or more languages, including Hebrew, Egyptian, Hittite, Hurrian, Indo-Aryan, Luwian, Greek, Phoenician, Aramaic, Assyrian, Babylonian, Persian, Latin, and Arabic. The urban population of Palestine was not international but cosmopolitan. That is, the non-Palestinian urban population came not just from other regions, but from the towns and cities of their respective regions. When rulers changed, the peasantry took little notice: the taxes, rents, and debts had to be paid as before.

WORK AND THE GODS AND GODDESSES

The modern divisions of work and home, work and leisure, work and education, and work and religion would have made no sense to a villager in ancient Palestine. Villagers started working in early childhood and stopped the day they lay down to die. Everything they did was a part of their work. Work was a given: necessary, natural, and virtuous. All aspects of work, which involved planting and harvest, soil and seed, rain, springs, and wells, and food and its storage, had the deepest religious significance to villagers, as these were the constant objects of their anxiety and devotion.

Working Groups.　An entire cast of village gods and goddesses, spirits, sprites, demons, goblins, and genies were thought to participate in the processes of production and reproduction. Every nook and cranny of house and field were inhabited by evil sprites who emerged from the earth at dark and returned to their dens at break of day. Their noises—shuffle and bustle, whispering and shrieking, hissing and cackling—were often difficult to distinguish from the sounds of animals, insects, and wind. A person had to be wary not to be fooled when a spirit assumed one of these mundane forms in order to deceive the careless. Magic was real, the evil eye a peril. The dead remained part of the community and reappeared to menace or console. Spells, sorcery, and divination "worked." Local saints and other odd persons offered services to be used and feared. Women who violated the patriarchal norm of what a woman should be were perceived as witches. A poor, old, childless, physically deformed woman might well be thought to envy households with healthy children, plentiful harvests, and thriving livestock. She was assumed to consort with dangerous spirits in lieu of establishing normal relations. Her services might thus be in demand to assist at childbirth, wakes, weddings, and other rites of transition. At the same time she invited caution, since she was also capable of causing grievous harm. Local saints ("prophets"), both men and women, whose belonging was in some way problematic,

26

were empowered to embody intervillage community identities broad enough to mediate competing claims of truth and power and the hostilities arising from them, and to attempt to channel the energies of the broader community, patrons and clients alike, for its betterment.

Like brokers and patrons, the gods, goddesses, spirits, demons, and genies had to be coddled, cozened, evaded, and thwarted, treated simultaneously with reverence and suspicion. The ceremonial of the village concentrated in thanksgiving feasts at harvests, of which barley, wheat, and the vintage stood out. The cult consisted mainly of service to spirits and holy men and women, alive and dead. It was practiced at household shrines in some corner or by the hearth or manger, or at a local shrine, situated by a numinous spring, tree, heap of stones, or tomb, and frequented by a local soothsayer, necromancer, prophet, or ghost. These courts in miniature, with their spirit-connected attendants, were the foci of favor, sanction, and jurisdiction for the various social groupings of and beyond the village.

Villagers knew the gods and goddesses of all Palestine—El, Baal, Athtar, Athtart (Astarte), Anat, Asherah, Dagon, Reshep, Shamsh (Shamash), Horon, and others—because they influenced production and reproduction as much as spirits and magicians did. But they were one mysterious force among many, and had to compete for the villagers' attention with local forces that exercised a more immediate influence in home, field, or well. Workers had little to do with the gods as kings, governors, and lords knew them. The rational specification of the roles of the various gods, the theory of their behavior and influence, the prescribed prayer service of their official cults, and the production and study of scripture were all activities sponsored by the cults of the elites. For workers the world of gods and spirits was the world of the village,

tent, and field: the unchanging care for work, the gains
and losses of production, the alternating dignity and
shame of social contact, the scarcely relieved hardship of
illness and debt, the capricious favoritism, the fatalistic
complaining and manipulation, whatever pertained to the
life of work.

Warring Groups. Not everyone worked at production
and reproduction. Noncultivators in the village included
heads of work teams who simply provided an ox, plow,
or some other means of production, lessors of such productive help, local small owners who could afford to hire
all the help needed to cultivate their fields, and officials
and agents residing in the village but representing outside
landowners. Wealthy families in towns and cities and on
their fringes did not work. Urban contrasted with rural
in that wealthy urban families were not able to raise food
themselves. They took their food from the villages. The
wealthy were the possessors of the firmest claims on the
lands of Palestine. They included kings, princes, warriors,
officials, administrators, and chief officiants of the religious establishments, as well as the chiefs, elders, and
warriors of the dominant tribes. These noncultivating
landholders were absentee landlords. They held lands of
villages, or more commonly extensive estates that engulfed villages, which provided the labor for working the
estates. If the estates had no villages, villagers were
brought from elsewhere to work them. The villagers who
cultivated village and estate lands rarely saw their absentee
lords, only the factors, troops, and toughs who showed
up to collect shares, taxes, rents, and debts.

The more land a household controlled, the less its members worked and the more they ate. Urban and tribal
landholders ate more and better food than villagers. They
had finer bread, better oil, better wine, more fruit. They
ate more meat and they ate it regularly.

Great landholders had more and better clothing than villagers. Besides woolens, they had linen and cotton garments, often made of imported textiles. According to one law in the Scriptures, urban priests got a sheep's first fleece, always the finest and longest the sheep would ever produce.

Great landholders lived in better housing. Their houses were bigger, and occasionally were constructed of dressed stone. Great landholders often had more than one house: elite households moved from locality to locality depending on season and whim.

With such advantages in nutrition, clothing, and housing, the landholding elite were generally bigger, stronger, and healthier than villagers. An early king of Israel, Saul, was said to tower head and shoulders above his peers. The town-dwelling Palestinians encountered by the migrating Israelites were described in the Scriptures' earliest history (fictional) as giants, in comparison with whom the average man was a mere grasshopper. The elite were less prone to illness and healed faster from injury.

Injury to the elite was not uncommon, since the chief activity of the male elite landholder was fighting. The overriding preoccupation of the elite household was enlarging its sphere of power in order to control the tenure claims to an increasing quantity of productive land and producing population. Whether a landholder was a charioteer, bowman, swordsman, administrator, merchant, scribe, priest, or temple musician, he was in the service of the ruling household or its great alliance or of households and alliances opposed to them. The main way for a ruler to stay in power or a landholder to expand his holdings was to fight for more. Fighting required arms, transport, provisions, supplies, moral support, and the steady hand of an assumed righteousness fortified by courtly literature, all of which were either acquired directly from the villages or indirectly in exchange for the village product at the disposal of the wealthy. Villagers provided not only the material means for this continuous warfare, but themselves as well. As noted, the struggle among the greats ramified through the ranks of patrons to the villagers, who were thus enlisted to support their own exploitation.

As with workers, the elite household was more than a domestic unit. It was the paramount social unit, the center of power through which the landholder as tax lord, creditor, and magistrate exercised authority. It was the structure through which he maintained his right to inherited property and status and defended himself or fought against others. For the elite, who did not engage in production, the household was above all a political organization. To enhance the household's political cohesion, family members, servants, clients, and hangers-on ate and drank together when practicable, and visited the same religious shrine.

Cults and Jurisdiction.   The service of a shrine's cult confirmed its jurisdiction, the right and power of the household's strongman as leading patron to interpret and apply local law safeguarded by the cult. Such law governed land use, credit, taxation, and tort. Public adjudication was carried out in the open, usually outside the town gate, town, or village, or in the village pen, since the cramped houses and alleys of settlements allowed little room for gatherings of more than a handful of people. Adjudication was a contest of power as much as truth, subject to the endorsements of the spirits and saints of the locale. Like land use rights, jurisdictions overlapped in complex patterns. With rare exceptions, jurisdictions were based on household power, and the meshing of jurisdictions was decided by the same alliances and contests that determined the power of households relative to one another. Might made right, and might meant the political house: enterprising, hard-fighting fathers, uncles, sons, and sons-in-law, and clever, robust, loyal, and fertile women. Such was the prime custom, and "custom, king of all mortals and immortals, led the way, justifying the most savage behavior with a high hand" (Pindar).

The cults of the elite expressed their benefactors' pre-occupation with armed coercion, conquest, and defense and with the administration of food collection, storage, and disposition. Baal was the divine guardian of this enterprise. Baal engaged in armed struggle, vanquished his opponent, built his palace, engendered his family, ensured favorable weather and the productivity of the land, and defended the established orders of society. Though no worker, he was a favorite of king and producer alike. El was chief of chiefs. He dwelled in a tent like a nomad, but often in highland or desert or by the sea—coastal or montane—on the paths of trade and travel where the tribe typically plied its power. Anat and Astarte were the divine king's consorts, sovereign, nubile, and magical. The chief El's consort was Asherah, who shared his predilection for the paths of the sea. Horon guarded the underworld, where many warriors were destined to reside. The favor of Reshep was sought to protect a fighter from sword, immolation, or fever in war. Shamash, the sun, ruled the sky and shed light on all activity above and below the earth, thus sanctioning true judgment in the kingdom of the gods and on earth. The cults of these gods and goddesses entailed prodigious quantities of meat, which was burned whole for their delectation or shared with the cult officiants or priests and sometimes offerers, those who were concerned that the gods eat as well as the royal court. Garments of fine cloth, utensils of bronze, gold, and silver, precious stones, and incense—in Palestine all products of

the foreign trade of the elite—played their role in the urban
cult.

The ruling elite were involved with the world of spirits
and sorcery, too, but with a slant suited to their military
and administrative occupations, and perhaps less fatalistic
than that of the lower classes. The service of the dead
was practiced by sodalities of warriors, who celebrated
their communion with departed heroes by feasting to
excess on the meat and wine, produced at cost to the
villagers, that strengthened their bodies and fortified their
wantonness. The favor of the spirits and demons of the
shrine as the place of judgment was sought to counteract
the vain complaints of clients and debtors who appealed
incessantly for justice and mercy without realizing that
larger projects were afoot in the world than their petty
pleas. The gods of Palestinian warriors became the gods
of Egyptian warriors in the days of the greatness of Egypt,
and the gods of Egypt made headway in Palestine as well.
For example, the besieging pharaoh appeared as Baal. The
same was true later of Assyrian and Babylonian gods in
the periods of their supremacy. The culture of the
wealthy—for whom expansion meant life—and hence
their cults as well, crossed the borders of war with ease,
especially beneath the banner of imperial command.

CHAPTER TWO

Egypt in Palestine

At the horns of the Fertile Crescent lay two great fertile river valleys, Egypt and Mesopotamia. These two valleys supported great populations using irrigation agriculture several times more productive than rain agriculture. Whenever a strongman of either valley succeeded in getting his forces together, he could extend his rule throughout and beyond the valley, establish his proprietorship of the state on a hereditary basis, and pass rule to his heir. Between these valleys, central Anatolia supported the great kingdom of Hatti (that of the Hittites) and northern Syria, the kingdom of Mitanni. The history of Israel began, as Alt recognized, as Egypt and Hatti were about to vie for suzerainty along the crescent between their kingdoms. It was Egypt that succeeded in taking over Palestine. For centuries before, during, and after the emergence of Israel, Egyptian strongmen and their commanders, fighters, and surrogate warlords marched up and down the lowland of Palestine and into the hills and imposed Egyptian rule.

Egyptian strongmen conquered cities in Palestine and through them coastal seaways and Palestinian land, to

obtain control of both trade routes and territory. Extant
Egyptian iconography of the period shows no less than
twenty-six examples of a pharaoh besieging and taking a
Palestinian city. Expansion secured Egyptian access to
trade and tribute and, more important, provided a buffer
against attack on the Egyptian homeland. The New Kingdom period, which began about 1550 B.C.E., witnessed
a sharp increase in both maritime trade and land trade.
The sea bore heavy traffic between the delta and the Palestinian and Syrian coast. On land, ass caravans journey-
ing to and from Egypt could number four hundred
animals or more. The king's court in Egypt received trade
and tribute in strategic and luxury goods locally insuf-
ficient or unavailable. Commodities included copper, tin,
timber, wheat, olive oil, wine, cattle, woolens, jewels,
slaves, nuts, and spices. Slaves and wood may have been
particularly significant, the latter for construction, car-
pentry, and fuel for smelting. In return the occasional
strongman of Palestine might receive local grain ship-
ments, protection, silver, luxury wares, garments, and
exotic items such as rare fish.

Copper and tin were essential for making bronze. Egypt
mined copper in the Sinai and the Arabah south of the
Dead Sea, partly with Palestinian workers and slaves, but
also traded for copper from Cyprus, the main source in
the ancient world. Tin came from as far east as Iran and
Afghanistan and as far west as Spain. From the east it
was shipped overland to Assyria, then up the Euphrates,
overland to the coast, and by sea to palaces all over the
eastern Mediterranean. Some tin was carried overland
from the central Euphrates through Damascus to Hazor
in northern Palestine. The forests of the Lebanon and the
Amanus mountains were the prime source of timber for
ships, palaces, furniture, bows, and other elite fabrications
in Egypt.

The eastern Mediterranean and its coasts were the scene of fierce competition and opportunistic cooperation by a variety of political, military, and maritime forces operating out of the main centers of trade. To control part of the eastern Mediterranean and upper Euphrates was to control a strategic sector of trade essential to the prosperity of any major palace. The palace of the pharaoh also controlled trade on the Nile and in the Red and Arabian seas. The central eastern Mediterranean came under the control of a set of Greek palaces in Greece and Crete. Hatti controlled central Anatolia and a set of vassal states in northern Syria. As Egypt and Hatti expanded during the fifteenth and fourteenth centuries, they came face to face in Syria.

TUTHMOSE III AND THE NEW KINGDOM

Near the end of the Middle Kingdom, approximately 1650–1550 B.C.E., Palestinian strongmen—the Hyksos—ruled Egypt and Palestine from Memphis and then Avaris in the eastern Delta. Their rule in Egypt was brought to an end by Kamose and his brother Ahmose (1552–1527), the founder of the New Kingdom. It took ten years to expel the last Hyksos king from Avaris, and another three-year siege to take Sharuhen, southeast of Gaza in Palestine. Ahmose's victory at Sharuhen ushered in the Egyptian New Kingdom empire in Palestine, a political order that was to last four hundred years and play an essential role in the rise of Israel.

The early New Kingdom military campaigns were isolated forays. Egyptian texts report that Tuthmose I (1506–1494) marched against Mitanni as far as the Euphrates. Tuthmose II (1494–1490) reigned only long enough to attack insurgent Palestinian tribes to the east. Archaeology suggests a more thorough disruption. Every excavated site in Palestine that was occupied between about 1550 and 1480 shows at least one destruction layer and often more during this time. Destruction layers have many possible causes, but the coincidence of so many probably reflects the disorder accompanying the setback of Palestinian forces during that period.

Tuthmose III (1490–1436) conducted military campaigns in Palestine and Syria every year for almost twenty years, starting about 1468. Each spring, when winter vegetation provided forage in the desert and the rains had tapered off so the expedition would not bog down in mud or marsh along the way, the pharaoh would gather an army, with chariots and their mobile bowmen to the fore, and march through the Sinai along the sea to Palestine. Once in Palestine, every village within striking distance of the highway was a potential target for grain supplies and fodder, as grain and hay harvests were reaching their peak at just this time.

Tuthmose III's first expedition confronted on the Orontes River in Syria a coalition of strongmen led by the ruler of Qadesh, eager to defend their privileges of taxation and jurisdiction. The battle line was drawn in Palestine, in the Jezreel valley near Megiddo, strategically located where the main track north through the Carmel ridge descended to the plain. Nearly all traffic on the coastal road from Egypt to Syria and points north and east passed this way. The Asian coalition fortified Megiddo, then went out to meet pharaoh in the field. Tuthmose prevailed. The defeated remnant retreated into the city, leaving their chariots and steeds, many trimmed with gold and silver, easy prey for the king of Egypt. The siege, the usual form of resistance and attack, commenced.

The siege lasted from May to December. The city was taken, and "the princes of this foreign country came on their bellies to kiss the ground to the glory of his majesty"

Tuthmose.[1] The victor forced the defeated princes and their men and families to transport his booty of silver, gold, lapis lazuli, turquoise, wheat, barley, sheep, goats, and cattle to Egypt. The wheat alone amounted to 11,000 tons, besides what the soldiers had looted. The sheep numbered 20,500 and the cattle 1,929. Plowing, which required cattle for traction, must have been a luxury in the region of Megiddo for years thereafter. In addition pharaoh took 340 live prisoners, 2,041 horses, 924 chariots, of which one was a ceremonial artifact made entirely of gold, 200 coats of leather mail, and 502 bows. He then assigned the annual produce of the fertile lands previously controlled by the sovereign of Megiddo and his allies to the Egyptian and Palestinian strongmen who pledged loyalty to him. They compromised a new urban elite obliged to pharaoh, who himself claimed ownership of the entire lowland region.

Tuthmose went on to plunder three more cities north of Megiddo—Yanoam, Nuhashe, and Halkur, which may have been under the rule of Qadesh. From them he collected among other things 1,796 slaves, with their children, numerous costly embellished bowls, jars, vessels, and utensils, 235 pounds of gold and silver in the form of discs ready for working, and numerous ornate chairs, tables, stools, statues, and clothing. In the king's own account, "the fields [of all these cities] were redivided into arable plots and reassigned to inspectors of the palace . . . in order to reap their harvest."[2] The king of Egypt thus assumed feudal lordship over nearly the entire Asian coastal lowland.

To uphold his claim, Tuthmose campaigned no less than a further fifteen times in Asia. His fifth campaign took him as far north as northern Syria. On that trip he got hold as well of two cargo ships, "loaded with everything, with male and female slaves, copper, lead, emery, and the rest." One rebellious town he destroyed "with its grain. All its pleasant trees were cut down. His majesty found the entire land of Djahi [Syria] with their orchards filled with their fruit. Their wines he found lying in their vats, as water flows, and their grains on the threshing floors. . . . They were more plentiful than the sands of the shore. The army overflowed with its possessions. . . . Now his majesty's army was as drunk and anointed with oil every day as if at feasts in Egypt itself."[3]

On his sixth campaign, Tuthmose destroyed this same town again, and Qadesh in similar fashion. As usual he took children of the town elites as hostages. "List of the children of princes carried off in this year: 36 men; also, 181 male and female slaves, 188 horses, 40 chariots." In his seventh campaign he secured control of ports up and down the coast. In "every port town," he crowed, he found bread, olive oil, incense, wine, honey, and fruit awaiting shipping—so plentiful that the scribe declined to list the quantities for monumental display "in order not to multiply words."[4]

Alongside tributary urban regimes, Tuthmose established a network of garrison cities to administer territory under Egyptian sovereignty. The chief Egyptian governors were stationed at Gaza, Kumidi at a major crossroad in the Biqa valley in Lebanon, and Sumur on the Mediterranean coast west of ancient Amurru, near present-day Tripoli. Joppa on the coast of Palestine was a major ordnance depot, along with Ullasa on the north coast. In all these cities except Kumidi, the local rulers were demoted or deposed and replaced by Egyptian officials. Palestine and the southern and central coast became one administrative district (Canaan)[5] and southern Syria, from Hazor north to Qadesh, another (Apu or Upu). The third district, farther north, may have been ruled differently. It seems to have been less effectively controlled and may not have been held to annual tribute. Egyptian troops and foreign mercenaries manned garrisons in many other towns in Egyptian-held territory. These included the Palestinian towns of Bethshan, in the eastern part of the Jezreel valley, guarding the main route linking Egypt with Syria and Mesopotamia, and possibly Yanoam.

The Egyptian governors were called residents or commissaries, or more generally the "great," or magnates. Local rulers were termed the mayor, king, "man," or *wer* (Egyptian, "magnate"). Egyptian governors and administrators required the rulers of vassal cities to collect tribute, provision Egyptian troops, protect trade, and supply *corvée* gangs to garrison cities for work in their incorporated agricultural territories. In the fourteenth century B.C.E., the king of Megiddo wrote to the king of Egypt, "May the king my lord be apprised concerning his servant and concerning his city. As for me, I am cultivating in Shunama and, as for me, am furnishing *corvée* workers. But look, the other city rulers who are with me are not doing as I. They are not cultivating in Shunama and they are not furnishing *corvée* workers. But I am."[6] These gangs also garrisoned the cities, defended their walls and gates, and repaired damages.

The administration of the Asian territories—the tax system, the treatment of crown lands as temple lands, and the use of Egyptian factors—was modeled on practices in Egypt. In Egypt the court depended on paramilitary Medjay tribesmen from the southeast to help keep the peace, and these were sent into Palestine and Syria for the same purpose.

The organization of crown lands is illustrated by the following account written under Tuthmose, already cited in part: "The fields were made into arable plots and assigned to inspectors of the palace . . . in order to reap their harvest. List of the harvest which his majesty carried off from the arable plots attached to Megiddo: 207,300 sacks of wheat . . ." This system seems to apply to at least the four cities taken in the great first campaign, and there is no reason to doubt that the pattern was repeated elsewhere and often. Other texts show that rulers in towns bordering crown arable bore responsibility for supervising gangs sent by rulers from towns farther away. Produce was transported to urban granaries, such as Joppa, expressly for provisioning Egyptian military campaigns. Some produce was probably also shipped to Egypt.

Such Egyptian royal estates existed near most of the towns of Palestine. Many towns were given Egyptian names, and it is likely that these, along with their lands, were expropriated in their entirety from local dynasts. Gaza, for example, was renamed by Tuthmose "That-which-the-ruler-seized." Other towns were named Tuthmose and later Ramesses and Merneptah. Before long Tuthmose dedicated Yanoam, Nuhashe, and Halkur, all localities in Asia, to the temple of Amon, four hundred miles up the Nile at Karnak, for payment of annual tribute.

The northernmost lands under Egyptian control were Amurru in the hills of present-day northern Lebanon, Qadesh on the upper Orontes, and Qatna just south of present-day Hamath. Late in Tuthmose's reign, his son Amenhotep led an expedition to the region north of Damascus. Two letters found at Taanak in Palestine and dating to the mid-fifteenth century may relate to this campaign. In one, an Egyptian named Amenhotep faulted the ruler of Taanak for not reporting to Gaza. In the second, he ordered him to show up at Megiddo with his fighters, ready to march. On this campaign seven defiant Palestinian rulers around Damascus were killed and their corpses displayed on the prow of the royal barge up the Nile and on the walls of Memphis.

AMENHOTEP II

In his seventh year, Pharaoh Amenhotep II campaigned into northern Syria as far as Aleppo "to extend his frontiers," pushing back the boundary with the king of Mitanni as far as possible. Proceeding "like Reshep," he put down a revolt at Ugarit and was received with respect in the Orontes valley. He returned to Egypt with 550 captured elite charioteers, 240 of their wives, 872 child hostages from ruling families in Syria and Palestine, and hundreds of chariots, horses, and weapons.

Although Amenhotep's chariot corps was considerably strengthened, the lasting effect of this campaign is unclear. Two years later Amenhotep felt obliged to return to Asia, but confined his campaign to Palestine. The control of later pharaohs extended no farther north than Qadesh. Amenhotep confirmed recognition from the rulers of Aphek and Yaham in the coastal foothills south of Carmel. Then he descended on the villages of two towns in the Sharon plain along the coast to the west and plundered their recently harvested grain stores. He took the two towns with no resistance and carried off everyone and everything in it, as slaves and booty for himself and his troops. A nearby town resisted. He captured it and took alive 34 oligarchs, 231 Palestinian fighters from the town and its villages, 54 chariots, each with one horse, and a throng of women, children, and property belonging to the Palestinians. A total of 372 Palestinians lost their lives in the encounter. From there Amenhotep led his battalion to Anaharath near the Sea of Galilee, plundered the town, killing 123 in the process, and took captive 17 elite charioteers, 68 other Palestinian men, 6 child hostages, 7 display chariots adorned with silver and gold, innumerable weapons, and some 800 head of cattle. He then piloted this monstrous drove back to Memphis.

Upon arrival, Amenhotep had his scribes list the captives as 3,600 *abiru,* 15,000 *shasu,* and 36,300 other Palestinian men, not counting the notables. The *abiru* (this term has other spellings in the literature, including *apiru* and *habiru*) are mentioned in over two hundred texts from the Fertile Crescent from the eighteenth to eleventh centuries B.C.E. The term referred not to a national or ethnic group but a social type or role. The one characteristic that applied to all *abiru* was that they had been uprooted from one political and social context and forced to adapt to another. An *abiru* was a migrant or displaced person in a new social location. These displaced persons originated mainly from two sectors of society, the village and sedentary tribal sector, about which Chaney's analysis is particularly illuminating, and the urban sector. Reasons for breaking former ties included war, famine, lack of opportunity at home, personal disaster, debt, excessive taxes, and lengthy military service. The poorest elements of tribes often broke off from home and kin and sought their fortunes elsewhere.

Although some *abiru* migrated singly and hired themselves out for service of some kind, most banded together in their new location to form independent gangs. These gangs became bandits, pillagers, or extortionists, or hired themselves as a fighting force to the highest urban or tribal bidder. The Akkadian equivalents of *abiru* meant killer, robber, and plunderer, as well as migrant. Bands of *abiru* usually consisted of a few members and one main leader, but in urban battalions groups could on rare occasion rise to a thousand or more. Service in a king's army or chief's militia could further a man's or squad's settlement in their new location through an established military career. *Abiru* often became adept at advanced military skills they may not have started out with. Within any particular group, members would begin to marry and the

gang to disintegrate before long. Thus the gangs rein-
tegrated themselves into urban or tribal society. *Abiru*
played a major role, for example, in establishing the dynastic state of Amurru.

The people called *abiru* in different places and times had
nothing more in common than their transitional social
condition. Each society had its own *abiru,* whose constituency was constantly changing. Local rulers were dis-
posed to hire companies of these migrant fighters: as aliens
they functioned outside the kin-based relations of power
in a given locality, and, if adequately compensated, they
remained loyal to their employer, fighting on his side
rather than his enemy's side. This use of *abiru* is particularly well illustrated by two identical cuneiform documents discovered at Kumidi, copies of a circular letter
from pharaoh to the rulers of Damascus and a town in
the Biqa. The letter requested the rulers to send *abiru* to
Egypt. The pharaoh planned to settle them in Nubia, in
exchange for comparable bands of fighters transferred
from Nubia to Asia. This exchange of alien mercenaries
illuminates pharaoh's attempts to control the local politics
of his imperial garrisons.

In the century after Amenhotep, *abiru* became a de-
rogatory term among Palestinian rulers for alleged renegades against pharaoh. Rulers and governors of cities sent
dispatches to pharaoh protesting their loyalty and complaining that neighboring rulers had rebelled and become
abiru, or that another ruler's troops were *abiru* attacking
the writer's city. The *abiru* were one of the many unsettled
factors in the conflicts between Palestinian cities under
pharaoh's sovereignty. As *abiru* they were by definition
alien, even when serving a ruler as a necessary fighting
force. Designation as *abiru* associated them by name with
outlaws and brigands. In the dispute between two cities,
the *abiru* who were troops to one ruler were renegades

to the other. Egypt did not mind its vassal cities exhausting their energies with struggles against each other rather than against Egypt, and Amenhotep II's 3,600 new *abiru* made a valuable addition to his own manpower. No doubt some were deployed back to Palestine following enculturation in Egypt.

Shasu was the word the Egyptians used for the tribal peoples of Palestine, some of whom were pastoralists, in texts covering the period 1500–1150 B.C.E. There are many fewer references to the *shasu* than to *abiru* in the Egyptian texts. Peoples called *shasu* covered a wide area, including Libya and the eastern Egyptian desert. One reference to the "land of the *shasu*" seems to refer to the Transjordan, another clearly to the highlands of Edom south of the Dead Sea. Some *shasu* were linked with the mountains of Palestine, others were described traversing the Sinai with their flocks and entering Egypt, and some are found in towns, as expected with tribal people. Most of the references to *shasu* involve military encounters (most of the sources in which they appear are on military subjects to begin with) in which like the *apiru* they operate as mercenaries fighting with or against the Egyptian army, or as paramilitary or bandit gangs. One pharaoh speaks of destroying their tents. The temple reliefs of Pharaoh Seti I described the *shasu* in the same terms used in another inscription of the same king for the *abiru*. In a letter from Damascus dated a century later, the Egyptian commissioner catalogued the forces behind him as "the royal archer, together with my troops and my chariots, together with my brothers, my *abiru,* and my *sutu*" (Akkadian *sutu* was the apparent equivalent to *shasu*). Gottwald has pinpointed a principal difference between the two social types: the *abiru,* uprooted and newly assimilating, were never identified by their native region, while the *shasu,* tribal and hence quasiterritorial, often were.

Amenhotep boasted that when the kings of northern Syria, Hatti, and Mesopotamia heard about his horde of booty, they fell over one another in the rush to send him gifts and tribute, "in order to beg peace from his majesty, seeking that there be given to them the breath of life." "We are under your sway, Amenhotep," they were said to avow, "for your palace rules in this land forever."[7] The kings of the great kingdoms of the Fertile Crescent may not really have acted this way, but, with pharaoh and his troops on the march, the kings and princes of Palestine did.

For two hundred years, the main superpower rivalry in the Fertile Crescent pitted Egypt against Hatti. During the fourteenth century B.C.E., the kings of Hatti grew in strength. In the thirteenth century, they conquered Mitanni and became the dominant power over the city-states of northern Syria. Their encroachment on the Egyptian imperial domain progressed until the great standoff at the battle of Qadesh in 1274 B.C.E., which later resulted in the détente that underlay Egyptian relations with Hatti for the second half of the thirteenth century.

THE AMARNA PERIOD

From the beginning of this period, the first half of the fourteenth century, comes an invaluable corpus of nearly four hundred letters written by foreign kings and Egyptian vassals in Asia to the foreign office in the Egyptian capital during a period covering the end of the reign of Amenhotep III and the reign of his son Amenhotep IV, known also as Akhnaten. The Amarna letters abound with complaints from local rulers about the lack of Egyptian support for their rule. In the fourteenth century Egyptian control in Palestine and Syria continued entrenched, and

Egypt's loyal vassals expected direct and immediate assistance in moments of crisis. Until recently it was thought the Amarna letters showed that Egypt lost its grip on Syria and Palestine during this time, when pharaohs made few if any military excursions to the northeast. It is now recognized that Amenhotep III and Akhnaten, far from neglecting their empire, kept close watch on imperial affairs and directed them from their capitals with little loss of authority and control. Needed materials were brought to Egypt by peaceful means, through commerce, gifts, and tribute. The Amarna letters refer to silver, copper, bronze, glass, wood, chariots, cattle, and slaves channeled to Egypt. On one occasion a certain Shubanda of south Palestine supplied five hundred cattle. Again the villagers in his area must have faced a critical shortage of cattle for years thereafter, along with the resulting increase in the incidence of debt. The king of Jerusalem claimed to have sent to Egypt by caravan five thousand shekels of silver and scores of slaves. The caravan was robbed before he wrote his letter, so it is not known whether he was telling the truth. There is no reason to doubt the sum. Milkilu of Gezer sent fifty persons on one occasion and two thousand shekels of silver on another.

The Amarna correspondence spotlights the Palestinian warlords' concern for their relations with Egypt. The Egyptian state was not in a position to impose uniform law and order over the entire imperial territory, so it engaged in a policy of divide and rule. For the first century and a half of the Egyptian occupation of Palestine, Egyptian administration was rudimentary and ad hoc. Administration was handed over to men in existing positions: commandants, commanders, charioteers, landholders, tribal and gang leaders, and couriers already on location. The Egyptians controlled the territory through the circuit of a designated officer, who in this role was called a circuit official.

The degree of Egyptian control varied. In lands on the margin of influence, strongmen could wield their own power over large areas. Abdi-Ashirta of Amurru was a case in point, though against him and his son Aziru, Egypt finally exercised a heavy hand. While Hatti and Mitanni fought it out to the north, Egypt cared only about confirming its influence along the coast from Byblos north to Ugarit, including Amurru. The ruler of Byblos, Rib-Hadda, warned the pharaoh that Abdi-Ashirta was forming his own independent coalition along Egypt's border with Hatti. Rib-Hadda took the occasion to mention his own, related hardships, brought on by Egyptian policy. The sale and indenture of his people to Egypt and the endless delivery of agricultural produce to Egypt left the farming population impoverished and the land with too few hands to work it: "My field is like a wife without a husband for lack of plowing." Under these conditions, he wished to impress upon pharaoh, the populace had every reason to defect to Abdi-Ashirta.

Abdi-Ashirta campaigned south from Irqata. He captured the provincial center Sumur and continued his march south as far as Byblos, which he left destitute but failed to capture. Diplomatic threats delivered to him the allegiance of towns farther south, including Beirut, Sidon, and Tyre. Mitanni attacked his rear and forced him into what was probably an anti-Hittite alliance. This move exhausted pharaoh's patience. The Egyptian king sent a battalion, which recaptured Sumur and corralled Abdi-Ashirta in the bargain. The rebel was promptly restored to his throne in Amurru. Such an able opponent could serve the needs of Egypt by holding its greater enemies at bay as well as, indeed better than, any other warlord. Clearly pharaoh's victory over a foe did not automatically mean the foe's end—quite the contrary. This event provides an important clue to the significance of the sole reference to early Israel outside the Bible.

Not long after his reinstatement, Abdi-Ashirta was killed on the home front. Confirming Egyptian fears, Hatti threatened to move into the vacuum. Rib-Hadda urged pharaoh to suppress Abdi-Ashirta's sons, but the Egyptian court saw worse threats than these highland chiefs. The rebel's sons took over where their father had left off and attracted support for their policy among pharaoh's advisers. One son, Aziru, was permitted to organize the cities under his rule into a buffer state, reassembling his father's alliance with little resistance. When Rib-Hadda's complaints out of Byblos continued unabated, Egypt had him ousted and murdered, and handed the town over to his brother, who allied with Aziru. Aziru paid his respects to pharaoh in Egypt in person.

Meanwhile, however, Aziru had been forced over to the Hittite side and was now about to serve as a fighting proxy for pharaoh's worst rival. Qatna, Nuhashe, and Qadesh joined him, when Egyptian aid against Hatti failed to materialize. By Aziru's own admission, it was Hittite aid more than Egyptian acquiescence that provided him with his throne. It seems that Aziru swore allegiance to Egypt and Hatti by turns and remained more or less independent. Hittite pressure came to bear on towns as far south as Sidon, and for a generation or more local rivalries between neighboring towns played out the superpower struggle in miniature.

Farther south, in the Palestinian hills, Labayu of Shechem, in the central Palestine highland, played a role similar to Abdi-Ashirta's, minus Hittite interference, which did not extend this far south for another century. Labayu led a coalition of towns and chiefs and imposed his command more or less from the coast to beyond the Jordan and from the Jezreel valley to the territory of Jerusalem, interfering continuously with the kings of Megiddo to the north and Jerusalem to the south. The kings of Gezer and of Gath in the plain of Sharon were, on and off, his allies. Strongmen without an urban base also played significant roles: Tagi, Shuwardata, Baᶜlu-Quradu, Baᶜlat-Ariyim. Labayu apparently had the king of Akko on the coast in his pocket as well. Akko represented a link between the two groups opposed to pharaoh's loyal vassals in north and south, the parallel highland kingdoms and alliances headed by Aziru and Labayu and their respective dynastic successors. Here was a force with which Egypt had to reckon in its own backyard. The independence of the dominant families in the central hills is a recurrent theme of the history of Palestine. The Egyptians made the best of the situation. Labayu laid waste three towns, expelled their resident landholders, and supposedly on pharaoh's behalf put the cultivation of their fields in the charge of neighboring sub-warlords, for the benefit of the Egyptian stores. Their own subjects were then required to work these fields. When Labayu fell in an encounter with a band loyal to Egypt, one of his sons succeeded him in Shechem, and another became ruler in Pella, in the Jordan valley south of Bethshan.

In the Amarna period every town in Palestine was a potential enemy to every other. Pharaoh heard their protestations and incriminations with equanimity, knowing that the fighting among them served his interests and that the victory of the stronger, so long as he did not rebel outright, in turn left the empire stronger. Local disruptions were just that. Egypt's main concern was Hatti.

EGYPT AND HATTI

In the late fourteenth century, during the reign of the famous teenager Tutankhamen, Hatti invaded Egyptian territory in Lebanon. The Egyptian army struck back the following year and took Qadesh. When the Hittites soon thereafter recaptured Qadesh, Tutankhamen's widow sued to marry a Hittite prince as a gesture of détente. The Hittites retreated from the Biqa, which then formed the frontier between the two powers for the generation-long reign of Horemheb. Hatti's expanding influence encouraged the expansion of Palestinian maritime trade with the Aegean and with Cyprus during the fourteenth and thirteenth centuries B.C.E. As pointed out by M. Dothan, the archaeology of Palestine during this period could fairly be characterized not as "Syro-Palestinian" in scope, but first "Canaano-Egyptian," and then even simply "Eastern Mediterranean."[8]

During the nineteenth and twentieth Egyptian dynasties, from 1300 to 1150 B.C.E., Egyptian administration in Palestine intensified. In the early thirteenth century, Seti I (1291–1279) reintroduced the royal expedition to Palestine. *Shasu* incited trouble in the Negeb and Sinai. The rulers of Pella and Hammath across the river from Pella harassed nearby Rehob and the important town of Bethshan and beleaguered the latter's garrison. Seti defeated the tribes, retook Gaza, and campaigned up the coast. From there he dispatched three divisions to put down the unrest in the eastern Jezreel and Jordan valleys. On a later campaign he engaged the Hittites in battle around Qadesh, which continued its role as meeting point for the two great powers.

Ramesses II (1279–1212) succeeded Seti I and ruled sixty-five years. By this time Egypt had extended its empire south into Nubia and Kush and organized its territory again along lines similar to those employed in the heartland of Egypt itself. Such strict integration was not possible in the northern parts of Egypt's Asian holdings, but under Ramesses II and his successors, Merneptah (about 1212–1202) and Ramesses III (about 1183–1152), the intensity of Egyptian occupation in Palestine reached a crescendo previously unknown in the New Kingdom period.

Early in his reign, Ramesses II fought against *abiru* near Bethshan, where he established his authority on a firm basis. The decisive encounter of his reign occurred in his fifth year of rule. At that time he engaged the Hittites at Qadesh in the largest set battle ever between the two forces. The battle was apparently a standoff. Hittite forces pursued Ramesses in retreat south as far as Damascus, however, and it took Ramesses five years to quell the revolts in Palestine inspired by the Hittite success. Relations between the powers continued strained until the accession of Hattusilis III, who, threatened on his eastern flank by Assyria, in or around 1257 signed a treaty with Ramesses II that remained nominally in effect through the rest of the century. The frontier was reestablished in central Lebanon. The text of the treaty is extant in similar though not identical Egyptian and Hittite versions. It consists mainly of a double set of clauses covering the extradition of rebels against the opposing crown. The preoccupation with border rebellion recalls the geopolitics surrounding Abdi-Ashirta's border maneuvers a century earlier. Now that the border had shifted south, the center of attention over pliable vassals and clients shifted to the region between Hazor and Qadesh.

PEAK OF POWER

The ostensible peace allowed one of the greatest periods of building by any pharaoh. Ramesses moved his capital to the former Hyksos capital in the delta and renamed it "House of Ramesses." In addition to Egyptian influence in Palestine, Palestinian influence spread in Egypt, due to the large number of Palestinians resident there in a variety of stations, and to the adoption of much of the Palestinian pantheon in Egypt. The thirteenth century saw a rising stream of customs and ideas flowing both ways across the "Way of Horus" in the Sinai.

From 1250 to 1150 B.C.E., Palestinians witnessed Egypt's greatest imperial strength in Palestine. The size and prosperity of many towns in Palestine finally owed more to Egyptian desire to turn them into Egyptian strong points than to local initiative. As the entry point to Palestine, Gaza, with its resident commissioner and his palace, had been a particular focus of activity. By 1200 it had been turned into a permanent Egyptian garrison, and its livelihood was based largely on its imperial role. Imperial expeditions provisioned themselves at Ashkelon. Joppa was a major center. During the last century of the New Kingdom in Palestine, the bustling Egyptian activity typical of Gaza and Ashkelon, described by the Egyptians as "maritime ports," was extended to other sites in southern Palestine as well.

Recent archaeological survey in the north Sinai has revealed the intensity of Egyptian development along the Way of Horus. Using draft labor, the Egyptian court, especially under Ramesses II, established forts, granaries, way stations, administrative centers, and industries, particularly mining. Over eighty New Kingdom sites have been discovered between Suez and Gaza, including several fortresses guarding the desert route. A granary with a forty-ton capacity was maintained midway across the Sinai. Forty way stations broke up the ten-day march. Twelve of these, from Sile at the edge of the delta to Gaza in Palestine, are described at the end of the papyrus Anastasi I, discovered in the nineteenth century. The Egyptians had stepped up their occupation.

Ramesses II planted his forces along the Way of the Sea from the Besor to the Yarkon, from Gaza to Aphek near present-day Tel Aviv. Aphek, on the eastern edge of the coastal plain opposite Joppa, formed something of a northern border of intense occupation, although Egyptians had a firm hold on Bethshan also, where the Jezreel and Jordan valleys merged. Ashdod was strengthened as a coastal supply base. Ramesses' Karnak reliefs show him besieging Ashkelon. Merneptah came to power at age sixty after his father's long reign and probably at most accompanied only one expedition to Palestine, early in his reign. This adventure may have earned him his epithet "subduer of Gezer." The Way of the Sea along the Palestine coast had now become an extension of the Way of Horus. Forts and supply points were located approximately every twenty kilometers at Gaza, Ashkelon, Ashdod, Mahoz, Joppa, and Aphek. The importance of the first three of these in later Philistine times was a reflex of this Egyptian policy.

By the reign of Ramesses III (1183–1153), Egyptian settlements extended southeast from Gaza along the Besor, the beginning of a road network leading to the Arabah and its copper mines and on to the southern Transjordan. Stations along this route included T. Jemmeh, T. el-Farʿah south, and possibly T. Masos, where a scarab of Ramesses was discovered.

Merneptah's domination of Gezer laid the groundwork for the extension of Egyptian power into the central and southern hills of Palestine. This began under Ramesses III, but was far from complete when the empire collapsed at the end of his reign. In the Judahite foothills, Ramesses III annexed Lachish, T. Seraʿ (probably Ziklag), T. Hesi, and possibly T. es-Safi (Gath). If the scant evidence for a Late Bronze Age Egyptian temple in Jerusalem is borne out, it would date to this period.

Egyptian involvement in Palestine reached its peak under Ramesses III. Egyptian policies and practices had an impact on administration, architecture, art, funerary rites, and cults. With indigenous labor the Egyptians built forts, residencies, and ceremonial city gates. They fashioned *stelae,* statues, and Egyptian ornamentation on existing structures. Palestinians found themselves increasingly beholden to the Egyptian law of the palace. Documents have been discovered detailing the imposition of direct Egyptian taxes.

The great towns of New Kingdom lowland Palestine entered the final phase of this period of their culture under the firmest imprint of the empire they had ever known. Ramesses III was a great builder of temples at home, and it occasions no surprise that he extended this practice to the provinces. Nine towns in Kush and Palestine were consecrated to the god Amun. Gaza had an Egyptian temple to Amun, Ashkelon one to Ptah.[9] Egyptian shrines at Bethshan were rebuilt. Some historians believe these Egyptian temples attest to an Egyptian concept of the whole of Palestine as the property of the Egyptian crown.

All known governor's residencies of Egyptian type were erected during Ramesses III's reign. These were carefully built mudbrick structures with thick outer walls. Such residencies have been found at T. Sera˓, T. Jemmeh, T. Hesi, T. el-Far˓ah south, T. Masos, Bethshan, and Aphek. At Aphek the Egyptian residence was erected on the site of the local Palestinian ruler's palace.

Lachish was annexed to Egypt under Ramesses III. His name appears on a scarab and on a bronze object found in the area of the city gate. Archaeologists digging at Lachish have also turned up bowls inscribed with administrative texts in Egyptian. One inscription refers to a harvest tax of a kind paid to an Egyptian temple. Remains of a twelfth-century Egyptian temple have been found on the summit of the tell, on the site of a disused Palestinian temple. Lachish, the second largest town in Palestine after Hazor, reached the height of its Late Bronze Age prosperity during the reign of Ramesses III. It was destroyed at mid-century and abandoned.

The findings at T. Sera^c were similar. A governor's residence was erected. Bowls with administrative notes record large amounts of grain brought as taxes. One is dated to "year 22," which must refer to the reign of Ramesses III.

While the reign of Ramesses III marked the zenith of the Egyptian occupation of Palestine, at the same time the territory under Egyptian control had shrunk by and large to the southern coastal plain and foothills. North and east of the Carmel ridge, in erstwhile Egyptian strongholds such as Megiddo and Bethshan, the intensity of Egyptian rule was diminished. The territory north of Bethshan was still less securely held. This was the Egyptian political frontier zone, which Egypt was obliged to place under the control of proxy forces left to develop as semi-independent allies.

Throughout the New Kingdom period in Palestine, the Egyptian court used local and foreign elites and mercenaries to perform its services. As typical in Palestinian history, small groups and individuals from all over resided in Palestine. In the Amarna period, Ashkelon had an Indo-European mayor, and Egyptian garrison commanders stationed in the pass between Megiddo and the coast had Indo-European names. They belonged to an elite class of warriors found throughout Syria and Palestine at this time, called *maryannu*. The fact that alien elites resided in the cities is further illustrated by the onomasticon of cuneiform tablets from fifteenth-century Taanak, where three-fifths of the names were Palestinian, one-fifth Indo-European, and one-fifth Hurrian/Anatolian. Foreign mercenaries and elites played a role in the few highland towns as well, where in Jerusalem in the fourteenth century a Hurrian king held sway. Later the Egyptians would employ other, non-Indo-European invaders and settlers from Europe and Anatolia (among them the Philistines) in similar roles. Since groups of elites took care to distinguish themselves from one another in every way possible, these alien elites maintained their names and languages and lent to the elite social landscape a distinctive cultural variety that in one more way set military and administrative classes off from working classes.

COLLAPSE

By the end of Ramesses III's reign, Egypt was ensconced in an expanding territory in coastal and southern Palestine. In a matter of decades after his death, however, practically nothing was left of the great empire. Historical records cease altogether, and archaeological evidence of Egyptian presence in Palestine diminishes to practically nothing by about 1130. The end of the New Kingdom in Palestine is conventionally marked by the reign of Ramesses VI (ca. 1141–1133), whose name appears on a bronze statue base at Megiddo. The occasional scarab or other small object appears later, but these only confirm the sharp decline that began around 1150. Egyptian mining in the Arabah and Sinai came to a halt. Over the entire eastern Mediterranean during the last half-century of the New Kingdom, great kingdoms and empires had come under pressure and collapsed. These included Hatti and the Mycenaean palace cities. Goods and services characteristic of interurban and interregional intercourse declined, in some areas dramatically. There is evidence of widespread famine. (The causes of general decline are the subject of debate and will be treated briefly in chapter 6.) Egypt was the last of the major states to collapse, and by no means the least.

Until recently it was widely believed that the fall of Egypt in Palestine and the boundary between the cultures of the Late Bronze Age and Early Iron Age occurred around 1200. This traditional dividing point still appears in introductory treatments, although as up-to-date works are published it will gradually be corrected. Historians now regard 1150 as a more accurate date for the transition (such as it was) in most places from the New Kingdom culture of Palestine to its successors, referred to archaeologically as the Iron Age. It has become inaccurate, therefore, to associate the emergence of Israel with the inception of the Iron Age. Israel existed at least two or three generations, and probably much longer, before the end of the New Kingdom and the Late Bronze Age.

During the middle third of the twelfth century, a new alien force replaced the Egyptians. It consisted of European and Anatolian masters later identified in Palestine mainly by the term Philistines. Their role in Palestine and their struggle with Israel over the inheritance of Egypt's empire in Palestine will be examined (chap. 5) after a further look at the decline of settlement during the New Kingdom in Palestine (chap. 3) and to Merneptah's reference to Israel and its meaning (chap. 4).

CHAPTER THREE

The New Kingdom Pattern of Settlement

Having clarified where and how Egyptian and other alien masters of Palestine, and their Palestinian surrogates and clients, lived in the New Kingdom period, it is time to examine how three hundred years of Egyptian suzerainty affected where and how the indigenous, working population lived. Over the ages the pattern of settlement in Palestine has varied with changes, especially political changes, in people's lives. Whether people lived in the fertile lowlands, the desert, the mountains, areas of poor drainage, the Judahite foothills, and other areas varied with changes in migration, climate, technology, suzerainty, and most importantly interregional political economy, such as the integration of the New Kingdom into the efficient trade and communication network that spanned the eastern Mediterranean in the Late Bronze Age.[1]

How settlement patterns are conditioned is particularly significant here because Israel became an established kingdom largely in the wake of one of the more dramatic settlement changes in Palestinian history: the settlement of villagers in what had been a sparsely inhabited highland during the twelfth and eleventh centuries, or Early Iron Age (see chap. 6). It is first necessary to examine the nature of settlement during the height of Egyptian imperialism, that period prior to the spread of settlement on the settlement frontiers of Palestine in the Early Iron Age. Where did the peoples of Palestine, including "Israel," live, and why?

During practically the entire three centuries of the Egyptian empire in Palestine, economic and political exploitation disrupted social relations and aggravated hostilities within the region. As a result, permanent settlement retreated from frontier zones and population declined. Only in the last half century of Egyptian rule did this trend reverse itself.

THREATS AND RESPONSES

Let us look again at what the working people of Palestine faced. The farming families of the towns, villages, homesteads, and tents of Palestine suffered the hazards of drought, flood, weeds, pests, and soil depletion. The inflexibilities of land tenure, taxation, and extortion increased the risks of production. The insecurity of village production induced farmers to reduce their risks whenever and wherever possible.

Risk reduction took several forms. A farmer, family, or village could shift the burden of risk onto a creditor by choosing tenancy, sharecropping, or even indentures in place of direct land tenure, though these alternatives were not usually chosen by the farmers. Or they could diversify further than usual into sheep and goat husbandry. Villagers normally practiced diversified subsistence production, itself a form of risk reduction made possible by the diversity of microclimates and ecological

zones in the Palestinian landscape. For subsistence economies, pastoralism was a low-risk form of capital development, an insurance against crop failure, a mobile form
of capital accumulation, and a means of evading taxes.
Pastoralism promoted more elastic community ties. Pastoral groups formed close-knit, sedentary villages, or dispersed, tent-dwelling, nomadic tribal units, or one of a
whole array of mixed variations between these two. The
farmer could even depart from the village altogether and
either relocate in the town for menial or military work
or into the hills as an outlaw, which might also involve
raiding and fighting. Though village work in itself was
honorable to the villager, life in the village held few at-
tractions. Sometimes emigration led a villager far from
his or her home. Under certain circumstances commodity
production provided an option for the town landholder
or wealthier villager. However, while it seemed to offer
opportunities for short-term relief for villagers, in the
long run it placed a heavier economic burden on most
farming families. Moreover, at the same time other villagers were moving into pastoralism to escape the hardships imposed on them by the spread of commodity
production, the intensification of land use resulting from
such production competed with pastoralism by reducing
pasture.

The cohesiveness of social groups at the village level
persisted despite the disruption caused by changes in residence or economic base. Productive roles were flexible.
There were few rigid social patterns tied to agriculture
or raising sheep and goats. The multiplicity of types and
combinations of subsistence economies and their relative
interchangeability meant that at one time a social group
could engage in one role and before long shift to another.
It was possible for small social units to disintegrate under
economic and social pressure, but more often they clung

together in a new economic and social configuration. The urban center in this system was one variable focal point among many. Urban rulers, warriors, and creditors determined prevailing tax and credit policies, but then had to react to and cope with the new rural socioeconomic configurations their policies induced.

The pattern of settlement typical of Palestine during the New Kingdom period consisted of urban centers three to twelve miles apart, each with six to ten associated villages and hamlets. Typically the rural population was no more than two or three times greater than the urban population. The economic and political insecurity of these urban domains discouraged agriculture and encouraged pastoralism. Large parts of the countryside were left uncultivated. The total product of the land depended on a lack not of land but of labor. The frequent references to *abiru, shasu,* and *sutu* attest to the indeterminate proportion of the population who prescinded from settled cultivation. Social unrest sprung from and fed into the struggles of one elite faction against another for the limited agricultural product owed their towns or to the Egyptian occupation. A portion of the urban population itself engaged in subsistence production.

The towns were small, usually on the order of five to ten acres, with rarely more than a thousand inhabitants and seldom that many. The social elite consisted of anywhere from perhaps a tenth to a quarter of this urban population. Except for Hazor, the towns of Palestine were considerably smaller than their north Syrian counterparts, mostly because arable was more extensive farther north, in the bulge of the Fertile Crescent. When Egypt in Asia was forced to hunch into Palestine alone, its loss was great. No wonder the imperial occupation reached its oppressive finale when it did, as Egypt attempted to squeeze the land

dry. The power of the elite was exercised through a network of personal and political ties centered in the palace
and temple. The main problem faced by the military elite
in the face of the fluidity of population was less the control
of land than of people. There was little point to com-
manding the taxes of a field if there was no one to farm
it. This problem the New Kingdom administration never
solved.

SHRINKING SETTLEMENTS

Given such social fluidity, the nature and patterns of settlement were fluid as well, along with the overall level
of population. Changes in settlement followed in relation
to other political and economic developments in Palestinian society.

In the centuries prior to the Egyptian occupation, Palestine saw one of its all-time great periods of urban and
agricultural development. The Middle Kingdom and Second Intermediate period in Egypt, during the twelfth and
thirteenth dynasties and Hyksos's rule (about 2000–1550
B.C.E.), brought with it in Palestine a steady growth of
fortified urban sites with large populations whose upper
classes were prosperous. Agricultural production was
abundant. This development was at its zenith between
1650 and 1550, when the Middle Kingdom occupation
was reversed and northern and central Egypt was ruled
by Hyksos lords and forces. These forces were based in
Avaris in the delta (T. ed-Dabᶜa) but were supported by
the strength of the urban military in Palestine itself.

The overthrow of the Palestinians by the founders of
the New Kingdom ended five hundred years of urban
growth. Avaris was destroyed about 1540. The New
Kingdom in Palestine saw a rapid decrease in the number
and size of settlements. By the middle of the fifteenth

century, the number of settlements was only a third of
the number a century earlier. Only seventeen of the
seventy-seven sites known from the period of urban
growth continued occupied until the establishment of the
New Kingdom in Palestine. On the coast, there were only
three such sites, an astonishing diminution. The dislo-
cation of population was severe. In the Middle Bronze
Age, the population of all of Palestine west of the Jordan
was roughly on the order of two hundred thousand. In
the Late Bronze Age it was half that. In the highland, the
decline was greater, to about one-seventh the previous
population. The size of the remaining settlements was
greatly reduced. Many contracted to small compounds a
fraction of their former size, situated in the highest section
of the former settlement. Ashdod, for example, shrank
to its twenty-acre acropolis. Except for late New Kingdom policy, it might have vanished altogether.

During the New Kingdom, new settlements tended to
be founded along the coast and the main trade way. The
highland and inner regions were largely deserted. Prior
to 1550, the highland supported several urban sites, including, from north to south, T. el-Farᶜah north, Shechem, Shiloh, Bethel, Jericho, Jerusalem, Beth-Zur
(northwest of Hebron), and Hebron. With the coming of
the New Kingdom to Palestine, most of these were abandoned or greatly reduced in size. Of ten sites occupied in
the earlier Middle Bronze period of growth, only Beth-
Zur, T. Marjameh, and possibly Jerusalem were left occupied. Gibeon and T. Rabud (Debir) had been the largest
sites, and both were abandoned altogether. During the
fifteenth century, Shechem was resettled, but Beth-Zur
was abandoned. In Shechem, under Labayu or his sons,
the main fortress-temple was rebuilt and continued in use
into the twelfth century. Nearly every hill country site in
the New Kingdom period was small in comparison with

lowland sites. Throughout Palestine the number of large settlements decreased sharply, so that by the fourteenth century their number was less than a fifth of what it had been in the Middle Bronze Age. Of six large sites, only Lachish survived for the duration of the New Kingdom period. Hazor was the notable exception to the decrease in site size, due possibly to the destruction of nearby Dan, and also to its location directly on the main route north and in a center of Egyptian activity prior to the thirteenth century. It remained abnormally large, more than four times the size of Lachish. Its destruction and abandonment, which apparently occurred in the first half of the thirteenth century, significantly altered Palestine's urban landscape.

Recent archaeological surveys of highland sites of the Middle and Late Bronze Ages bear out this picture of population shift or decline. Zertal found 116 Middle Bronze II sites in Manasseh, Finkelstein sixty such sites in Ephraim. These figures shrink to twenty-one and five respectively for the Late Bronze Age, representing ratios of six to one and twelve to one respectively. Only Bethel flourished in the central highland in the latter part of the Late Bronze Age. All together the hill country from the Jezreel valley to Beersheba shows about two hundred sites during the Middle Bronze II in contrast to between twenty-five and thirty during the Late Bronze II. In other words, the number of settlements in the hills in the period 1750–1550 B.C.E. was approximately seven times greater than in the period 1400–1150. When the entire area west of the Jordan is included, the drop in total population was not so drastic, since the coastal plain, southwestern foothills, and northern valleys maintained their population in the Late Bronze Age. As already noted, between the Middle and Late Bronze Ages the population overall fell by half.

Most of the settlements of the New Kingdom period, including large and strategic sites, were unfortified. Only a few were surrounded by a wall during even part of the period. Hazor again stands out against the rule. There, during the entire New Kingdom period, use was made of the earthen rampart that had defended the city prior to 1550. The general lack of fortification was a conspicuous departure from the norm of urban defense in the region, especially considering the Cyclopean dimensions of the typical Middle Bronze Age defensive installation. The absence of walls during the New Kingdom probably resulted from Egyptian policy, which, following the destruction of so many existing town walls, called for preventing the construction of new ones.

Toward the end of the fourteenth century, town life began to recover, but only in certain areas. At first, sites that were to be reoccupied were depopulated and impoverished. Recovery came after about 1400. By the thirteenth century and the reign of Ramesses II, the sheer number of occupied sites had returned to pre-1550 levels, but the area where they were located, their size, and their populations were still greatly diminished. The percentage of small or medium sites remained the same during the entire period, dropping only slightly by the time of Ramesses II. However, the number of tiny settlements increased fourfold, and this increase is what kept the overall number the same. However, the total area of all settlements occupied during the reign of Ramesses II was less than half the area of *all* the settlements of the pre-1550 period of growth, covering nearly five hundred years. The real reduction in area was thus considerably less than half, to perhaps a third or quarter of the previous area. The total area of occupation in Palestine in the thirteenth century was extremely small when looked at in historical perspective, and tiny to medium settlements constituted more than ninety percent of the number. Clearly the population of thirteenth-century Palestine was a fraction of what it had been three hundred years before, and the patterns of production and social relations had been transformed. In Gonen's words, this period was a time of "dramatic weakening of the urban fabric."[2]

The settlement pattern that developed during this period is a further important part of the overall picture. In the highland during the fourteenth century, Dothan, a very small site (two and one-half acres or less), along with T. el-Far'ah north, Bethel, and Jerusalem, all small sites (from three to twelve acres), were reoccupied. North of Jerusalem, T. el-Jib (Gibeon) shows a burial site from this period, but whether this indicates a contemporaneous settlement is uncertain. Bethel, guarded by remnants of its earlier wall, became the major site of the southern highland. Excavations at Bethel have uncovered houses from between 1400 and 1200 that were among the finest examples of domestic architecture in Palestine until much later. During the same period, Shechem was apparently less populous than before, even though, as we have seen, the Amarna letters show that Labayu, attempting to profit from the trade on the coastal and valley route to Damascus, controlled Shunem in the Jezreel valley and Gath-Padalla in the Sharon valley and harassed Megiddo until his murder. Gatu was a similar renegade operating out of the hills near Bethshan. Judging from the Amarna letters, in which Bethel surprisingly is not mentioned, Jerusalem was the other main political center. T. Rabud, the only medium-sized site (twelve to twenty-four acres), was also reoccupied in the fourteenth century.

During the thirteenth century in the highland, T. Rabud was again abandoned, as was T. Marjameh. Jenin was settled, an indication that some agriculture was spreading into the most accessible part of the hill country toward the end of the thirteenth century. This area became the focus of some of the earliest highland village settlement in the Iron Age. Hebron was probably also occupied, but so far only burial remains have been uncovered. Hazor (until its destruction) and Lachish continued as the largest settlements in Palestine. There is no evidence for any settlement in the Negeb.

COASTAL STRENGTH

Even though by the time Ramesses II came to the throne few of the pre-1550 sites remained occupied, the last century of the New Kingdom saw only limited activity in establishing new sites. New sites were of two types: new harbors on the coast to the north, and the Egyptian strongholds in the southern plains (see chap. 2). No new harbor was founded along the coast south of Joppa, but north along the coast a string of new sites appeared, to supplement the few small ports from the previous era: Rosh Haniqra, Akzib, T. Abu Hawam, Shiqmona, T. Megadim, and T. Girit. These harbors served the trade with Cyprus, Mycenae, and other ports in the eastern Mediterranean.

The second type of new settlement was the Egyptian stronghold. These were established in increasing numbers in the fourteenth and especially thirteenth centuries. Almost all were located in the southern coastal plain, the heartland of Egyptian presence in Palestine. As already noted, the Egyptian fortresses at Deir el-Balah, T. el-Farʿah south, T. el-ʿAjjul, T. Jemmeh, T. Mor, Jaffa, Aphek, and Bethshan continued the chain of fortresses on the coastal route across the northern Sinai and helped Egypt tighten its hold on southern Palestine and the trade way leading north. If these strongholds are subtracted from the total number of settlements in New Kingdom

Palestine, the result is an even more acute decline in settlement and population, lasting right through the thirteenth century.

The manifest result of the Egyptian occupation during almost its entire duration was to restrict and reduce settlement, agriculture, and population growth. As Egyptian garrisoning and taxation increased, the incentives for farming diminished. Many villagers, individually and in families and groups, became more dependent on the credit of the lords, became wage earners, indentured servants, or slaves, shifted further into pastoralism, or left the town or village altogether to join pastoral bands or pursue careers as brigands or mercenaries in other localities. It may be no accident that the references to *shasu* and *abiru* seem to increase as the New Kingdom occupation wore on. Settlements along the southern coast and coastal highway survived, as long as the Late Bronze boom in tribute and trade in the eastern Mediterranean lasted. Otherwise village settlement throughout the region was chronically constricted.

The same picture applies in the Biqa valley north of Hazor toward Qadesh, where Egyptian influence and the hostilities fostered by the superpowers had a similar effect, although the size of Hazor may indicate some exceptional factor. In areas accessible to Egyptian control in northern and central Transjordan, the settlement history is again similar to western Palestine. The collapse of several Middle Bronze sites is attributed to the conquest of Egypt, even though Egyptian control in the Transjordan was never so intense as in western Palestine. In the Late Bronze Age, towns occupied at least ten sites in the northern and central Transjordan, in the Jordan valley, and around Irbid and Amman. These sites exhibit the same Palestinian culture, quality of finds, and cosmopolitan mix as in western Palestine. In contrast, settlement in the southern

69

Transjordan was sparse during the Middle and Late Bronze Ages.

The constriction of village settlement and population reversed itself dramatically within a generation of 1200 B.C.E. At that time there began to appear in the north-central highlands of Palestine an extensive spread of villages and agriculture into areas that had been unoccupied for most of the preceding three hundred years. In many cases these settlements occupied and farmed areas that had never previously been occupied. The spread of settlement into the central hill country covered areas that two hundred years later would be the agricultural heartland of the monarchic state of Israel.

An entity known as Israel existed prior to this reversal of settlement pattern, and not all new settlements later belonged to monarchic Israel. It is therefore necessary to examine what the name Israel referred to before the location of Israel in hill country villages, the circumstances that attended the change in settlement through the revival and extension of villages, and the conditions that led to Israel being located in the hill country. What factors allowed highland settlement after 1200, although they had prevented it before, and how was Israel involved in the new settlement?

CHAPTER FOUR

Israel in the
Thirteenth Century

When first attested, Israel was neither a single religious group, family, nation, race, nor ethnic group. As far as is known, Israel began as a Palestinian tribe or tribal confederation (a difference in modern terminology) in the New Kingdom period. It was a name for power. Moreover, even in the thirteenth century B.C.E., the name Israel did not mean the same thing to everyone to whom it supposedly applied.

It was long thought the main problem in explaining the origin of Israel was matching the biblical accounts of a family arriving from Mesopotamia, Egypt, or the desert fringe and turning into a nation with the evidence of archaeology. Now it is clear that the Bible describes not the origin of Israel, but what some later court writers thought was the origin of Israel, on the basis of ideas and experiences belonging to their own time and place. The Bible therefore cannot be used to explain the origin of Israel through an accurate historical narrative with precise names and dates. The Bible tells much about what was happening in Palestine in the tenth century and later, thus setting the problem addressed by this book, but little about what happened before then, except for social circumstances, place names, names of political figures, and the location of shrines, all of whose exact historical relations remain unknown. Though such information from the Bible has its importance, it cannot be the starting point for the history of early Israel. Today biblical history must be analyzed as a function of Palestinian history, rather than the other way around.

THE MERNEPTAH STELA

One must start with the only written reference to early Israel outside the Bible. This reference appears in the last stanza of a series of commemorative hymns describing Pharaoh Merneptah's victory over Libyans in the fifth year of his reign. The current best estimate is that Merneptah's fifth year was 1207 B.C.E. The most this date might be off is ten or twenty years too late. The hymns, of which only the last deals with Palestine in addition to Libya, were inscribed on a *stela* discovered in Merneptah's mortuary temple in Thebes in 1896. It is sometimes referred to as the "Israel" *stela*.

This reference to Israel is at least one generation, and probably several, earlier than the extensive settlement of highland Palestine. It shows that in the thirteenth century B.C.E. Israel was a military force to be reckoned with, and that Israel was not named for a town. In the twelfth and eleventh centuries, people named Israel inhabited recently founded villages in the highland. Since Israel was a force before there were many highland villages, it appears to have become a mostly highland grouping only after it was politically established.

These conclusions may seem modest, but they go a long way toward clearing up the supposed mystery of the origin of Israel. Before Merneptah there is no information whatever about Israel. However, intelligent guesses can be made. Tribal Israel may have gone back to the fourteenth century or earlier, although it is not mentioned in the Amarna letters (no specific tribes are) and nothing definite can be said about it at that time. For Israel in the thirteenth and twelfth centuries, on the other hand, a hundred years and more before people of Israel began writing historical documents, these few lines of poetry provide valuable clues, when understood in relation to what is known about this period and similar circumstances in other periods of Palestinian history.

The Merneptah text says:

> The chiefs are thrown flat and say "Peace!"
> Not one of them lifts his head among the border enemies.
> Libya is seized,
> Hatti is pacified,
> Gaza[1] is plundered most grievously,
> Ashkelon is brought in,
> Gezer is captured,
> Yanoam is made nonexistent,
> Israel is stripped bare, wholly lacking seed,
> Hurru has become a widow, due to Egypt.
> All lands are together at "peace":
> Anyone who stirs is cut down
> By the king of Upper and Lower Egypt, Merneptah.

The stanza concerns the pacification of the empire's borders. Libya to the west and Hatti to the east and north are subdued. On the near side of the border with Hatti, Hurru (much of Canaan) is bereft: its gateway Gaza and, from south to north, the towns of Ashkelon, Gezer, and Yanoam and their territories are contained. Along the border with Hatti, Israel is ravaged. The name Israel is accompanied by a sign indicating that it does not refer to a town, as the other names do.

In the last decade a number of historians, following Frank J. Yurco, have begun to think that certain reliefs at Karnak in Egypt, previously thought to portray Ramesses II attacking Palestinian towns, may actually portray Merneptah, Ramesses' successor, and the apparent campaign described in this short last stanza concerning Merneptah's victories in Palestine. This interpretation is however uncertain. Redford and others have pointed out that the poem itself does not read like the account of a real campaign. Furthermore, there is no other evidence that Merneptah could have attacked all these places during his ten-year reign. Merneptah, who suffered from poor health, campaigned on the northern Mediterranean coast in his third year. This is the only time he could have campaigned at length in Asia before his fifth year, when he went west rather than east. His expedition into an area far north of Palestine suggests that Palestine itself was under control. As far as is otherwise known, conditions in Palestine during the decade of his rule were peaceful. The hymnic stanza referring to Israel appears to reflect the conditions of a more or less secure Egyptian administration. While Merneptah might have sent soldiers to Palestine during his first year or two to display imperial muscle, the campaign implied by the *stela* inscription may never have occurred.

It also remains uncertain whether the Karnak reliefs portray Merneptah instead of Ramesses II. Redford observed that Merneptah's poetic stanza is of a type of composition in which a city, building, statue, or relief inspires a stylized interpretation. In this case, it is an interpretation of Ramesses II's reliefs as though the reliefs applied to Merneptah. Thus the Karnak reliefs did portray a campaign of Ramesses II, as always thought, but then later, in Merneptah's reign, served as the inspiration for a summary stanza describing an imaginary campaign by Merneptah. Redford then noticed that since Israel is the only name in the text without a readily identifiable pictorial equivalent on the reliefs (questioned by Yurco), while the *shasu* are the only element on the reliefs not specifically named in the text, Israel and the *shasu* are apparently to be matched. The group Ramesses II's pictographer depicted as *shasu,* consisting of the type of people Seti I's and Ramesses II's scribes called *shasu,* was referred to by Merneptah's scribe a generation or two later as Israel. Israel was Merneptah's way of referring to a significant group of Palestinian *shasu.*

This indication of the tribal nature of premonarchic Israel fits with what little else is known, especially from the Bible. All the names in the stanza except Israel are accompanied by a sign that defines the name as a town or town-state. With Israel, the scribe used a sign that seems to mean "people." Moreover, whereas a territory, town, or town-state would be feminine in grammatical gender, Israel is a "he." The scribe thus juxtaposed Israel as husband to Hurru as wife. The scribe considered Hurru to be Palestine in general. He understood Israel as a body of people descended from a male eponym, not a territory or city-state. If the poetic figure of Israel as husband bore any relation to historical conditions, the political integrity of much of Palestine depended on Israel's viability.

TRIBES IN PALESTINE

To explore this reference to Israel and the nature of Israel in the thirteenth century, it is necessary to say more about tribal organization in ancient Palestine on the basis of better-known parallels. As indicated in chapter 1, tribal organization was essentially a concept of political identity and relationship among individuals and families, and between their chiefs and the state, in the face of the extreme injustice and insecurity that characterized Palestinian society. The concepts of tribe, clan, and so on referred to real relationships and had social and economic significance, but such relationships were highly variable, and the basic meaning of such concepts was political—having to do with relations of power. Tribal structure and membership were not permanent, but changed constantly, depending on the particular political and social environment. Tribal members made up a hierarchy of rule, alliance, clientship, and loyalty separate from the order of a state, although tribal heads could end up as rulers of a state. Tribal and urban elites were often closely associated, sometimes one and the same.

The political purpose of tribal identity was to mobilize and rationalize collective political behavior in opposition to some threat. The paramount threat, which gave the tribe as a political form its potency, persistence, and usually sharpest definition, was the state—at least in theory—whether in the tribe's territory or elsewhere. Opposition could be real or not, the rhetoric heightened or subdued, but the ethos of the tribe conveyed in principle a fundamental aversion to the state. The tribe thus offered an alternative to state political organization, sometimes compatible with the state and sometimes antithetical to it. The contrast between tribe and state was a reflex of the state's militant claim that political relations throughout a given territory could and should be uniformly ordered. Thus the state could attempt to project a national identity that assumed a political consensus of the populace. The tribe as a political metaphor was one way of embodying the real political complexities that the state's assumption of uniform order could not address.

The tribal concept of social order expressed a primary loyalty among the putative heirs of a common patrilineal founder, in preference to or to the exclusion of the loyalties required by the state. As far as the tribal member was concerned, the claims of the state, unless they represented the interests of a ruling house within the tribal organization, were secondary or illegitimate. The ability to follow through on the tribe's prior claim to loyalty depended on the power of the tribe relative to the state, and was extremely variable. Where the tribe was weak or had little leverage against the state, the opposition naturally was attenuated and minimized.

Tribal relationships were conceived in terms of kinship. Tribal kin relations did not extend far in actuality, however, only in the fictive conception of tribal members, and often not even there. Tribal identity was based on the concept of segmentary lineage, or shared patrilineal descent. Theoretical descent from a common patronym, in the form of a branch on an ancestral tree, created a relationship of equality, which was ideological, among all descendants at a given level of descent. Tribal idiom usually referred to three or four parallel levels of descent and relationship. The terminology for these levels varied, but they were the levels for which English terms such as household or family, extended family, lineage, clan, tribe, and tribal federation or alliance have usually served as approximations. These levels and relationships expressed the political relations and activity among elements of the tribe and between the tribe and the rest of society.

Practical notions of relationship took on substance in the world of ongoing political and social interaction. Alignments and affiliations shifted often. One recent study of second-millennium Mesopotamia and Palestine prefers ethnicity to tribalism as a social category. It notes the interactional character of social identity, and accentuates the communication of self-perception and the response of others in real social situations. This emphasis is correct. The relational import of the language of tribalism was an essential element, for example, of the interaction implied by an assertion such as Merneptah's that he had "annihilated Israel," which as a statement of fact was a clear impossibility. Ethnicity, however, is not a suitable category for understanding early Israel or ancient tribal organization in general. It continues to beg the question of the nature of Israel, particularly in its variability, by implying a singularity and a continuity with later Israel, which are commonly presumed but improbable and misleading. The changing practical definitions of tribal self-identity governed factional alignments over land rights, marriage strategies, feuds, patronage, and other activities. In tribally organized groups, power, leadership, and resources were all given definition according to current membership in a locally defined, changeable descent group.

Many such definitions, however, may have lain at most times in abeyance. The underlying purpose of the ideology of segmentary lineage was to cope with what Meeker terms "the threatening uncertainty of political relationships." For most tribesmen, because rigid loyalties posed a threat nearly as great as the state's, tribal identity came into play only in the face of a particular threat and was otherwise latent. Meeker cites Montagne, for example, among others regarding "the vagueness of all intertribal and intratribal relationships within the North Arabian tribal confederation, while insisting on the role of the tribal chiefs as political architects."[2] Again, the tribal position with the greatest degree of definition was that of chief. And it was the chief who dealt directly with the persistent dominating social threat, the power of the state.

Given the genealogical conceptuality of parts of the Hebrew Scriptures and the tendency to adopt that conceptuality in historical discussions of early Israel, it is essential to stress the primary political dimension and rhetorical nature of the language of tribal organization. The theory of a particular lineage or politically affiliated group rarely if ever matched biological descent. A group usually included members who were not related genetically or by marriage. The claims of a common patronym and the segmental lineages based on such claims were essentially putative. They changed over time, while of course biological history did not. The periodic reassessment of tribal relations took place in domestic negotiations, at local saints' shrines, and in the face of critical threat. Temporary ritual alliances were formed on such occasions as well.

Every tribal member and family was enmeshed in multiple, sometimes conflicting, nontribal affiliations and alliances. The tribe and its subsections embodied one organizational principle among many, in a complex and always changing political environment. Other principles of alignment and action might enhance or undermine the tribal alignment. These included faction, class, gender, age, the official or administrative definition given by the state, language, and especially jurisdiction. Sometimes tribal organization complemented and reinforced these alternative identities. Usually it ran against them. Monarchs, strongmen, gang leaders, brigand chiefs, resistance fighters, and outlaw sheikhs recruited in opposition to and in service with the ruling sovereign on the basis of many different organizational principles. Tribal identity, however, was one of the pervasive bases for local group recruitment, and tribes themselves regularly possessed a paramilitary sector.

The tree metaphor of descent supported an egalitarian notion of tribal identity. Tribal elites thought of themselves as egalitarian, and took many decisions collectively, or made them appear to be collective, when possible. But rarely if ever did such egalitarianism exist. The idea of segmentation supported the greater power of particular strongmen in the tribal group. At each level of organization, the segments were ranked according to their actual power. Whether articulated or not, everyone in the tribe knew who had more power and who had less. The sheikh of the highest ranked segment typically held the position of highest leader. Conversely, the segment pertaining to the man who functioned as highest leader took over the role of highest ranked segment. Compliance with the tribal elite conception of rank and hierarchy was sanctioned through much the same terror, coercion, and brutality practiced by the state elites, and conceded through the same indifference, submission, passive resistance, and desperate shortsighted fervor practiced by the nontribal populace.

Tribal heads worked for themselves as much as for the tribe. They elaborated the tribal ideology, or had it elaborated by a compliant poet or wise man, to solidify political alliances with members of other tribal groups and to enhance their own position in relation to state authorities, with whom they often cooperated. Tribal heads reinforced their privileges through their concepts of the tribe, which they spread through the ranks. The notions of tribal identity held by ordinary members of the tribe often diverged widely from the ideologies devised by the tribal heads. Meeker's study of one typical tribal group showed that "only the structure of low-level relationships was clear to the ordinary tribesman. He had some idea about the relationship of groups in his own vicinity, but not much more than this. The tribe had no precise structure as a political community. The tribal chiefs appear as the only men who had views about the architecture of the tribal confederation."[3]

The tribal strongmen typically ruled over their followers as landholders, military commanders, and judges, and allocated land to followers, even where the state made its own claim on the land. Heads of tribes were often involved in tax farming of both tribal and nontribal villages. In one attested case, the sheikh received a third of all tribal produce, though it was not unknown for him to confiscate more. The strongman administered the customary law of the tribe through the heads of the clans allied with him, his sons, other close relatives, retainers, and slave assistants. There was no rule that stated tribal heads had to like or respect the farming populace of their own tribe; the opposite was probably more common.

At the same time that tribal organization was structurally opposed to the state, it often worked for the state as well. The state typically appointed tribal strongmen, commanders of significant paramilitary bands of tribal fighters, to administrative positions, responsible for security of travel, collection of taxes, and jurisdiction and law and order on tribal lands or in tribal territory. The state often played an important role in the creation of the tribal elite, even without formal appointment. The power of the single strongman, commander of troops, or tribal squad leader resulted in part from the patronage of the state. The countervailing tendency was for the state, or patron, to divide and rule, fostering fragmentation among a set of clients and gang warfare within the tribal block. Tribal politics tended to be fragmentary in the absence of a strong external central force. A strong tribal head gained power and became established through trade, urban associations, state sponsorship, or state position.

How people have conceived of a tribe has reflected the way state administrations have approached tribes. States frequently assumed that tribes had a corporate identity they did not in fact possess, and gave to tribal strongmen authority and privileges that were an extension of state organization as much as of the tribe's concept of leadership. As a defined organization with a set structure of leadership, the tribe existed only as a function of state conceptualization and administration. This is the form in which the notion of tribe nearly always occurs in the Hebrew Scriptures, or any ancient writing, since virtually all ancient writing prior to the Hellenistic period came from the state. Thus the fanciful notion that early Israel permanently consisted of twelve named tribes remains extremely widespread even today (sometimes only by implication). In the process of helping to define tribal leadership, including who the leaders were and what they did, the state in its own interests frequently misconstrued the multiple political purposes of the tribal group as a whole. Because of their connection to the state, tribal leaders often considered the tribe as part of a larger tribal federation, but such larger groupings existed primarily as an extension of state policy, as a political and ideological framework in which major regional alliances were maintained. In actuality, the multiple chiefs of the different levels of tribal organization were often in competition or conflict with each other, and with chiefs who ranked above and below them. Meeker again finds his experience matching that of Montagne and comments that "tribal chiefs, as political architects, represented the confederacy in accordance with the intertribal conflicts of the moment."[4]

Tribal organization could be found in all variations of productive order and habitation. From villagers with few flocks through villagers who practiced transhumance, from nomadic, tent-dwelling pastoralists who farmed often and sometimes settled in villages to pastoralists who raided, traded, or fought for the state for their food, from peasant to king—all these could think of themselves in tribal terms. Tribes were in any case never isolated economically, but integrated into both village and urban economies. The tribalism described here owes much to Rowton's analysis of what he calls "enclosed nomadism" in "dimorphic" societies. Because nomadism was practiced on a continuum with settled life, however, and because the primary distinction that defined tribes was political rather than economic or ecological, Rowton's terms, with their suggestion of polarity, have not been widely accepted. The salient "polarity" in the history of tribes existed not in some systemic and constant feature of tribal culture in contrast to nontribal culture, but in the conflict between rival strongmen, tribal or otherwise, which was constant in Palestinian society.

TRIBAL ISRAEL

The presence of tribalism in the thirteenth century B.C.E., however, must have been related to the sociocultural fluidity of the village population of Palestine in the New Kingdom period, and its tendency, demonstrated by the reduction in settlement and population, to shift toward pastoralism and less settled patterns of production. As the percentage of people less attached to arable under state control grew, the opportunity for them to organize sociopolitically in opposition to the state grew as well. It was out of some of these people that the group subsumed, and taxed, under the political title "Israel" formed. However, many members, possibly most, of this Israel were villagers and town-dwelling farmers and day workers who had no special history of either pastoralism or political withdrawal. They belonged to "Israel" solely as clients in a particular political network conceived in tribal terms, which at this time happened, with Egyptian reluctance and support, to be growing.

Finkelstein suggests two kinds of archaeological evidence for pastoral groups in Late Bronze Palestine, corresponding to the *shasu* and *sutu* of the texts, with which Israel could be identified.[5] The first consists of sanctuaries isolated from permanent settlements or close to them but outside their bounds. These include sanctuaries at T. Deir Alla in the Jordan Valley, Shiloh, T. Mevorakh, T. Balatah at Shechem, and the Fosse Temple at Lachish. Such sanctuaries are not known in periods of high urbanization. Where the faunal remains of such sanctuaries have been analyzed, as at Shiloh, they show an incidence of sheep and goat bones consistent with a pastoral mode of existence. At Shechem and Lachish, sanctuaries were found within the settlement as well as outside. Such a pattern could be explained as serving the needs of a separate group of people residing outside the city bounds. Finally, most of the sanctuaries were located in areas of marginal settlement, where pastoralists might have predominated. The second kind of evidence is the Late Bronze cemeteries isolated from permanent settlements. These again are found mainly in frontier areas of little settlement.

Some scholars believe it is erroneous to assume that pastoral nomads leave little evidence of settlement per se. Clear evidence of nomad encampments has been found for the Early Bronze, Middle Bronze, Iron (tenth century), Nabataean, Byzantine, and early Arab periods. The fact that little such evidence has shown up for the Late Bronze Age suggests to some researchers that pastoral nomadism was not common at that time. This disagreement probably springs from the different ways the evidence can be interpreted. The kind of evidence Rosen points to pertains to nomad populations during times of significant urbanization. This circumstance must be related to the apparent lack of such evidence in the Late Bronze Age, since other evidence points to a significant pastoral component in the life of Palestine's Bronze Age population. Knauf finds the evidence points to groups such as the Shawawi of Oman: small and tiny groups of herders in the hills, with small and tiny ranges, without an expanding tribal organization. The essential point, however, is that evidence for nomadism is not required for locating thirteenth-century tribal Israel in Late Bronze settlements of northern Palestine.

The Merneptah stanza lumps all the tribal forces its author found it appropriate to refer to in his apparently imaginary evocation of Merneptah's triumph over Palestine into the single term Israel. Since Israel is the only tribal organization mentioned, the impression is given that Israel did in fact comprehend all such forces. Of course Merneptah's agents did not make contact and agreements with all tribes or even whole tribes in Palestine, only with a strategic chief or chiefs. It was in the chiefs' interest as well as Merneptah's to conceive of the tribe as a unity, making the most of the ideology of segmented lineage. The tribe was thus not referred to, as often tribes were, as the "sons of Israel," but simply as "Israel," the single putative ancestor of all tribal members. Israel was strong, as befit a tribe or tribal alliance with the name "El (the chief) commands (the tribal military)." Against a major force such as Egypt and its allies, the main tribes of Palestine might have wished at some point to be represented by a single tribal head, but the single term ought not to obscure the temporary political conditions, relating to the changing nature of Egypt's sovereignty in Palestine, that produced it.

The Merneptah *stela* does not reveal whether tribal Israel consisted of villagers or tent-dwellers or both, peasants or pastoral nomads or both, bandits or mercenaries or both, and so forth. These are incidental to the primary political meaning of the tribal conception. That thirteenth-century Israel was a tribal force likewise says nothing about whether it was based in an urban or rural setting, though the evidence of the *stela* suggests that Israel did not claim an urban base. Instead it reveals Israel as in concept a formidable tribe or tribal alliance, a tribal military force to be reckoned with, the kind of organizational definition that rulers can work with. As explained above, such a concept played a significant political role at the points of contact between Egyptian policy and tribal politics, both internal and external. Israel was in the first instance a political conception shared by both tribal leaders and the Egyptian administration. Israel was not a single homogeneous entity, except in the sense that virtually anyone might have had reason to oppose the state and hence to adopt a tribal identity. Israel was a political term more than a kinship, ethnic, cultural, or linguistic term, although it had implications in all these areas. It is extremely unlikely that Merneptah's Israel included the same set of tribes, or tribal designations, as those under Saul's or David's rule two hundred years later.

The substance of tribal identity, however, varied greatly from subgroup to subgroup. The unity of the term Israel was, like any such term, a myth of the interaction of Merneptah's agents and Israel's strongmen. This unity masked the complexity of the tribal order, with its confusion of hostilities and alliances. Israel was an expansionist, variable tribal system, carrying out tribal imperialism comparable, for example, to the well-documented instance of the Nuer of the Upper Nile in the nineteenth century, and possibly with Abdi-Ashirta and Labayu and their sons, assuming they practiced tribal politics. While there might be clues in the histories of similar movements, nothing certain can be said about the causes of the expansion and increasing power of Israel in this period other than resonance with the increasing power of Egypt. What is certain is that Israel was a political designation that emerged in importance in the mingling of imperial and tribal politics in northern Palestine.

Israel, then, was the way Merneptah's scribe identified the tribal *shasu* and other Palestinians shown on Ramesses II's or Merneptah's reliefs as operating in his own time, and the way he encompassed them within Merneptah's sphere of pacification. Bits of evidence combine to locate the heart of the presumably broad territory of this Israel in the north of Palestine. It has already been suggested that while *shasu* appeared in many places, the particular concern of Seti I at the beginning of the thirteenth century focused on those in the hills around Bethshan. "The foe belonging to the *shasu*," his propagandist wrote, "are plotting rebellion. Their tribal chiefs are gathered in one place, waiting on the mountains of Hurru," as also in the Merneptah *stela*. "They have taken to clamoring and quarreling, one of them killing his fellow. They have no regard for the laws of the palace,"[6] just as expected of tribal people. The captions on the reliefs depicting Seti's campaign linked his march against the *shasu* with the Palestinian hill country called Upper Retenu: "The return of his majesty from Upper Retenu, having extended the frontiers of Egypt. The plunder which his majesty carried off from these *shasu*, whom his majesty himself captured in his first year."[7] The sequence of localities named in the Merneptah stanza runs from south to north and concludes with Israel, thus near the Sea of Galilee or farther north. According to Finkelstein, the hill country settlement associated with Israel in the twelfth century apparently proceeded in general from north to south. In the later monarchic period, the heartland of Israel was always located in the northern section of the central highland. Pella has been identified as a possible source of resistance to Egypt.

Since each indication by itself is uncertain, together they are inconclusive. Nevertheless they are suggestive, and poetic indications of an "origin" of Yahweh in Edom (Deut. 33:2; Judg. 5:4; Hab. 3:3) do not necessarily contradict the suggestion for the thirteenth century. The location of Israel in the north of Palestine fits the most likely reason Merneptah's scribe mentioned them at all: the tribal elite of Israel and their paramilitary forces functioned as an extension of Egyptian military control in the buffer zone along Egypt's border with the Hittite sphere of influence, just as did Abdi-Ashirta and Aziru of Amurru. Egypt's overriding interest in Asia had all along been in Asia's role as buffer territory: the best defense is a strong offense. In the thirteenth century, the presence of Egyptian officers north of Bethshan clearly diminished. As *shasu*, Israel constituted a threat along the route to the north. What better way to control the threat than to digest it into the imperial order? Service in border and buffer zones has been the commonest reason in the history of Palestine for the administrative support of tribal strongmen and their hosts, and for state promotion of tribal alliances, all typically erratic in their loyalty. A few of the numerous examples that could be cited include the relations tribalists had with Assyrians in the Negeb and Sinai in the seventh century and with Greeks in the fifth and fourth centuries, and between Romans and tribalists on the Syrian border during the empire; the support of the Ghassanid kingdom by Justinian and the Lakhmid alliance by the Persians; and the many cases detailed by Sharon and Abu-Husayn for early modern Palestine.

The Merneptah stanza claims that Israel has been annihilated. Obviously Israel was not annihilated. In terms of political reality, unless the text is sheer fantasy it could only mean that Merneptah brought Israel under his control, as he did the towns named in the stanza. Israel's leaders were either neutralized, as Egyptian protégés, agents, or clients, or replaced. It would be interesting to speculate about the relationship of the Israelite tribal elite to Hazor, at this time defunct. The tribal elite may also have turned over taxes as tax farmers of villages, including tribal villages, they controlled. Like other local rulers, they may have had to supply *corvée* from villagers for the farming of Egyptian crown lands in the vicinity of Bethshan or Hazor. Given the nature of tribal politics, this was not a contradiction of the tribal structure's opposition to the state. Again, the tribe as a whole undergirded the power of the tribal elite at the interface of tribe and state. Israel as a force was not only a creation of both its tribalists and Egyptian New Kingdom policy—it was an arm of Egyptian power.

Another hint that Israel's elite chiefs and priests were related to Egyptian imperial control is that in the tenth century the prime chief of Israel and others associated with him in the time of a certain Ramesses were remembered as having Egyptian names. (There was an unbroken succession of Egyptian kings named Ramesses during the entire early Israelite period.) These chiefs and priests included Moses, later associated with the cult of Dan in the vicinity of Hazor, Aaron, Phineas, Hophni, Merari, and possibly others. (Phineas's name, meaning "swarthy" or "black," indicates he may have been a black African; other leaders of early Israel with Egyptian names may have been black too.) Although these names are few, they belong to apparently important individuals. Moses' traditional place of burial in the hills northeast of the Dead Sea suggests that he may have been a chief of Israel after the beginning of the emergence of highland villages in the twelfth century.

Why did these chiefs and priests of tribal Israel have Egyptian names? The power of the single strongman in tribal society was a function partly of consensus politics among the strongest elements in the tribal block, but also of a power struggle within the block and of patronage from the state. The form of state patronage in New Kingdom Palestine is clear: Egypt removed hundreds of Palestinian elite sons and daughters to Egypt to be raised there as hostages and socialized as loyal Egyptian servants and clients. A standard motif of Egyptian reliefs of sieges of Palestinian cities shows the besieged princes offering their children from the city walls to the conqueror as hostages. A tomb painting of the vizier of Tuthmose III shows Palestinian princes presenting their tribute in Egypt, including "the children of the princes of the southern [that is, Palestinian] districts . . . who were brought as the best booty of his majesty . . . to fill the workshop and to be serfs of the divine offerings" of his god.[8] Amenhotep II in one campaign brought back to Memphis some 2,000 Asians, among whom were 232 rulers' sons and 323 rulers' daughters. In other words, one-fourth of his captives were elite hostages. These were brought up in Egypt and then frequently returned to Palestine as rulers loyal to Egypt. In an Amarna letter from the Palestinian prince of Gaza and Joppa, the prince avers, "When I was young, pharaoh brought me to Egypt, where I served the king my lord; I solemnly stood in the city gate of the king my lord." Following a second campaign, Amenhotep II brought back in addition to princes themselves 3,600 *apiru*, 15,200 *shasu*, and 36,300 *Hurru*, with all their goods, sheep, goats, and cattle. Many Palestinian proxies for Egyptian administration were brought up in Egypt, though they often kept their Palestinian names. That Moses kept his Egyptian name indicates his Egyptian derivation and pro-Egyptian position, though he may have been Palestinian in origin.[9] He might have been one of the Medjay tribesmen sent in to police the Egyptian realm, or the son of such a tribesman born in Palestine. Or he might have had an Egyptian name simply because he was an Egyptian, an ambitious, adventuresome prince or tribal renegade of the Nile.

Israel's relationship to Egypt was as complex and changeable as tribal relations always were. Moses played a double role of loyal ally and rebel to pharaoh. Border forces were susceptible to defection on their own side and bribery from the other. Hittite fighters are attested in Palestine right into the period of the Israelite monarchy. Both mercenaries and employers were perennially unreliable. It was said that Aqiili Agha, a bedouin strongman from Egypt set up in northern Palestine under Egyptian occupation there in the nineteenth century C.E., was "a marauder when in rebellion and a man who lived off the villages by protection at other times."[10]

Given the decrease in overall resources in Palestine during the later New Kingdom, an increase in factionalism is likely and expected. It is safe to assume factionalism grew, though there is no direct evidence for it. All we have, thanks to Merneptah's propagandist, is a reference to a single tribal Israel, since, for both Egypt and the most powerful of the tribal heads of northern Palestine, it was more useful to publicize the mask of unity and political agreement than the reality of inciting one strongman against another in the attempt to neutralize them both. If the head of this unity at some time between Merneptah and Ramesses VI is known to us, his name was Moses.

At least some of the Israelite tribal elite were *abiru* in the sense that they were aliens in Egypt or, as Palestinian elite with long-term residence in Egypt, aliens in Palestine. As proxies for Egypt in Palestine, the tribal elite were displaced mercenaries. Moreover, many of the tribal members were displaced persons, uprooted from town,

village, or homestead as a result of the decline in settlement and production and their need to make a living
elsewhere in the border turmoil between the great powers.
On these grounds, apparently, the term *ibri,* or "Hebrew,"
was adopted into Israelite tribal culture, if *ibri* comes from
abiru, as most historians continue to believe possible. The
typical Israelite tribal leader was a client *abiru*-ite, or
"alienite," an identity that traced back to tribal Israel's
significant displaced population and official Israel's proxy
role, roots that were forgotten within only a few generations. The terms *shasu* and *abiru* were not mutually
exclusive. In the thirteenth century B.C.E., chiefs of Israel
could have been both. And of course the designation Israel
was far from inclusive. Thousands of non-Israelites in
Syria and Palestine were *shasu* or *abiru* or both.

The compact between Egypt and Israel lasted in one
form or another until David. With the collapse of the
New Kingdom about 1150, Philistine lords took the places
of their Egyptian counterparts and renewed their long-
standing threat to Egypt. In the struggle between the
Philistines and Israelites, Egypt presumably took Israel's
part more than the Philistines' part, to the degree it was
able, for the same reason it supported rebel movements
against the house of David in the tenth century. Some
early Israelite rhetoric preserved in the Bible may be hostile toward Egypt, such as the song of Miriam in Exodus
15; but most is not. The intensity of hostility toward
Egypt expressed in J, the history of Israel written in the
court of David, is a measure of how strongly this upstart
Philistine-backed monarch had to weigh in against the
custom of amity or collusion between Egypt and the chiefs
of early Israel, whatever the thrust of early Israelite ideology. The southern Judahite pastoral tribal story of flight

from Egyptian *corvée,* the exodus, was the tradition adopted by David for flattering his Negeb tribal allies and highlighting his anti-Egyptian stance. As explained further in chapter 7, it had nothing to do with the origin of Israel.

CHAPTER FIVE

European and Anatolian Rovers and Settlers

The tribal block Israel was not the only force in Palestine with which Egypt had to come to terms. Another important force consisted of warlords, rovers, mercenaries, and settlers from the Aegean area, including Greece, Crete, western Anatolia, and Rhodes, in part by way of Cyprus and the eastern Mediterranean coast. The Egyptians called such people "sea peoples," because many did in fact move around the eastern Mediterranean in ships, especially before they gained power in Syria and Palestine, but also after. Many did not. Moreover, in the popular study of early Israel, the phrase "sea peoples" has evoked images of migrations from nowhere comparable to the popular image of Israel's migration out of the desert: in this image, the encounter of the Philistines and Israelites pitted people from some mysteriously fecund "sea" against people from some mysteriously fecund "desert."

MORE OUTSIDERS

One way to keep in mind that these were aliens from somewhere is to call them Europeans and Anatolians, or

Europeans for short. Egypt dealt with many groups of such Europeans. For Palestine the most important were the Philistines, who ended up settling in the southern coastal plain and most of the contiguous lowland and making such a lasting impact that they gave their name to the land later called Palestine.[1]

An analogy, albeit imperfect, might help to explain the situation. Like the ancient Egyptians, the twentieth-century British had to deal with two important groups in Palestine: Hussein and Abdullah and their fighters, and the Zionists and their fighters. To the village majority, both groups were outsiders. The former were comparable to Israel's rulers, seen as tribal and holding the central hill country as the empire withdrew. The latter were comparable to the Philistines, who came from Europe, settled in the lowlands, and achieved dominance as the empire withdrew. Other quite accurate analogies to European or Anatolian intrusion include the crusading European elite who overran Syria and Palestine by land and sea in the twelfth and thirteenth centuries C.E., the Turks who ousted the Egyptian Mamluks in 1516–1517, and the combined European and Anatolian forces that ousted the Egyptian Ibrahim in 1839–1840.

More pirates than traders, and operating on land as well as sea, the European rovers included military adventurers similar to the Vikings and Crusaders. This was the age sung about by Homer (centuries after the event), when bands of roving warriors sailed in ships to seek their fortune in battle against cities along the coasts and in inland valleys. It appears they often ended up unattached to home ports in the Aegean and without ties to home folk. Some of these groups appear in texts as early as the fourteenth century. Some were Mycenaean, by no means the last fighters from Greece to menace Palestine in the biblical period.

Odysseus's tale of disguise to Eumaios exemplifies their activities. Home for only one month after the war, Odysseus claimed, he set sail again to plunder Egypt. Having arrived in the Nile,

I urged my eager companions to stay where they were, there close to the fleet, and to guard the ships, and was urgent with them to send look-outs to the watching places; but they, following their own impulse, and giving way to marauding violence, suddenly began plundering the Egyptians' beautiful fields, and carried off the women and innocent children, and killed the men, and soon the outcry came to the city. They heard the shouting, and at the time when dawn shows, they came on us, and all the plain was filled with horses and infantry and the glare of bronze, and Zeus who delights in thunder flung down a foul panic among my companions, and none was so hardy as to stand and fight, for the evils stood in a circle around them. There they killed many of us with the sharp bronze, and others they led away alive, to work for them in forced labor. . . . At once I put the well-wrought helm from my head, the great shield off my shoulders, and from my hand I let the spear drop, and went out into the way of the king and up to his chariot, and kissed his knees and clasped them; he rescued me. . . . There for seven years I stayed and gathered together much substance from the men of Egypt, for all gave to me.[2]

It would be a serious mistake, however, to think of these Europeans as mere pirates. Even the Vikings had a huge land base. The Hittite court knew their Aegean rivals as the Ahhiyawa or Ahhiya, probably Homer's Achaeans. In the mid-thirteenth century, during Ramesses II's reign in Egypt, the Ahhiyawa established a kingdom in southwest Anatolia and began to suborn and raid the districts on the Hittite border to the east. Hatti invaded Cyprus to stave off an Ahhiyawan takeover there. The king of Ahhiyawa formed a coalition with the king of northwest

Anatolia. Together they pushed the Hittite border farther eastward, biting off piece after piece of the empire. They plundered Cyprus during the reign of the Hittite king Arnuwandash, but his successor was able to recapture it. The Hittite court's preoccupation with its western marches encouraged the Assyrians to advance against them from the east.

Arnuwandash's contemporary in Egypt was Merneptah. Merneptah and Arnuwandash remained on good terms, in accordance with the remarkably long-standing treaty made earlier in the century by Merneptah's father Ramesses II and Arnuwandash's grandfather Hattusilis III. During a period of famine, Merneptah even shipped grain to Hatti. The reason for their détente is clear: both found themselves under military pressure from the European warlords and rovers on the move, and from the Assyrian echo to their movements. Their only hope for survival was to make up their differences on their common border.

Under these circumstances, Israel, the tribal alliance fostered by the Egyptian side in the buffer territory between the Egyptian and Hittite empires, continued to be deprived of leverage they might otherwise have acquired to play one side against the other, as had Abdi-Ashirta and Aziru in the preceding century. As long as Egypt and Hatti held out united against the onslaught of the Europeans, together they were able to prevent Israel from expanding between them. However, as first Hatti and then Egypt were overpowered by Europeans in Syria and Palestine and had to retreat from their mutual clasp, the chiefs of Israel, their batteries charged from having been plugged into the imperial system, sprang loose from the imperial pincers and empowered the tribal farming families beneath them to spill into the agricultural frontiers not yet ruled by the Europeans. This movement will be examined in detail in the next chapter.

EUROPEAN GROUPS

Many groups of European rovers are identified in texts from the later New Kingdom period. The Philistines were only one such group. The main rosters of Europeans come from Merneptah and Ramesses III, whose hardened occupation of Palestine was designed as a defense against, among others, the European onslaught. Many references to particular rover groups also occur earlier, especially in the accounts of the battle of Qadesh. In that battle, Aegean and Anatolian fighters on the side of the Hittites included the Arzawa, the Dardany (Homer's Dardanoi of Troy), and the Kashka, none of whom were among the "sea peoples" encountered by the Egyptians, and the Lukka, or Lycians, who were. Lukka pirates were famous in the eastern Mediterranean for almost two centuries. A fourteenth-century king of Cyprus, for example, wrote to pharaoh, "Does my brother not know that every year the Lukka people take another small town away from my people?" They came from southwestern Anatolia. When later Greek historians mentioned Carian pirates, they were probably referring to the Lukka. They appear again as allies of the Libyans against Merneptah.

The Sherden, or Shardana, fought on the side of the Egyptians. They are mentioned in the Amarna letters in the fourteenth century and the Ugaritic texts of the fourteenth and thirteenth centuries B.C.E. They later gave their name to Sardinia. They had attacked the Nile early in Ramesses II's reign, much as in Odysseus's tale. Ramesses defeated the attackers and incorporated them into his army. They fought at Qadesh with special status, and played a prominent role in Egyptian pictures of the battle.

Merneptah was pressured by several Aegean groups allied to the invading Libyans, in addition to the Lukka and Sherden. The Akawasha may also have been related

to Homer's Achaeans. They made up the largest contin-
gent of Libyan mercenaries. The Tursha came from Anatolia and are mentioned in the Hittite archives. They were
later linked with the Etruscans. The Shekelesh are known
from a letter from the Hittite king to the last king of
Ugarit, who presided over the fall of Ugarit to the European invaders. The letter refers to a man taken prisoner
by the Shikala, "who live in ships." Some of these Shikala
may later have settled in Sicily and given it their name.

Ramesses III faced a similar attack by Libyan raiders in
his fifth year. The Sherden again fought beside him, joined
probably by the Shekelesh. Some of the other groups
defeated by Merneptah might have joined them. In Ramesses III's eighth year, European rovers attacked from the
sea.

> As for the foreign countries, they made a conspiracy in
> their islands. All at once the lands were on the move,
> scattered in war. No country could stand before their
> arms. Hatti, Kizzuwatna, Carchemish, Arzawa [Cilicia],
> and Cyprus. They were cut off. A camp was set up in
> one place in Amurru. They desolated its people and its
> land was like that which has never come into being. They
> were advancing on Egypt while the flame was prepared
> before them. Their league was Peleset, Tjeker, Shekelesh,
> Denyen, and Weshesh, united lands. They laid their hands
> upon the lands to the very circuit of the earth, their hearts
> confident and trusting: "Our plans will succeed." I or-
> ganized my defenses in Palestine. I prepared before them:
> princes, commanders of garrisons, *maryannu*. I caused the
> Delta to be prepared like a strong wall with warships,
> transports, and merchant-men. They were manned en-
> tirely from bow to stern with brave fighting men, and
> their weapons. The troops consisted of every picked man
> of Egypt, they were like lions roaring on the mountain
> tops. The chariotry consisted of runners, of picked men,
> of every good and capable chariot fighter. . . . As for those

who reached my frontier, their seed is not, their heart and their soul are finished for ever.[3]

This marks the end of the Hittite empire. The Egyptian empire hung on for one more generation. However, like Israel, whose seed also, according to Merneptah, "was not," these attackers did get through and did last, to settle in the midst of the Egyptians along the Philistine plain. The Peleset were the Philistines. Some historians have suggested they may have fought on Ramesses III's side as well as against him. The Tjeker (a text from Ugarit appears to indicate the term was pronounced "Sikala" or "Sikela") came from Anatolia and later, according to Greek tradition, settled in Cyprus, where they founded Salamis. An Egyptian document from about 1050 B.C.E. locates them at the port of Dor on the central Palestine coast. There they raided offshore shipping, with a fleet of eleven ships, comparable to Odysseus's raiding fleet of nine ships. The Denyen were the Danuna of the Amarna letters, whose settlements grew just north of Ugarit, in the present-day Hatay. They may have been the same as the Danaoi in Greek legend. It is even possible they were related to the Israelite tribe of Dan, since the earliest reference to Dan in the Scriptures questions why, in the battle against the chariots celebrated by Deborah's song in Judges 5, Dan stayed in their ships rather than joining the fray. The Weshesh are otherwise unknown. Ramesses III did not mention the Tursha, but a Tursha chief was shown among his prisoners.

These same groups also attacked by sea:

As for those who came together on the sea, the full flame was in front of them at the river mouths, while a stockade of lances surrounded them on the shore. They were dragged ashore, hemmed in and flung down on the beach, their ships made heaps from stern to prow and their goods wasted.[4]

In the reliefs of this great battle, the Europeans were portrayed under migration with their families, belongings, and livestock. They trekked in two-wheeled ox-drawn carts. Their oxen were humped zebu, known in Anatolia and Mesopotamia but not previously in Palestine. Three of the attacking ships on the sea front are manned by fighters wearing the same headgear as the defenders of the ox-carts in the land battle. The raiders' boats resemble Syrian trading vessels of the fourteenth century B.C.E. and later. Although many rovers migrated in whole families, they included a significant aristocratic component, as indicated by their success in battle.

In a supplementary account, Ramesses III boasted,

> I extended all the boundaries of Egypt. I overthrew those who invaded them from their lands. I slew the Denyen in their isles, the Tjeker and the Peleset were made ashes. The Shardana and the Weshesh of the sea, they were made as those that exist not, taken captive at one time, brought as captives to Egypt, like the sand of the shore. I settled them in strongholds bound in my name. Numerous were their classes like hundred-thousands. I taxed them all, in clothing and grain from the store-houses and granaries each year.[5]

Not by coincidence, Ramesses III immediately went on to describe a victory over tent-dwelling *shasu* of Edom. His control of Palestine was henceforth largely a function of his relation to these two groups, European migrants and Palestinian tribesmen.

The Shardana were retained as mercenaries in Egypt. The Peleset, or Philistines, were accommodated, probably by necessity, in Palestine, and gradually settled in the coastal plain and elsewhere. As Egyptian control collapsed about the mid-twelfth century, these "Vikings" took over the mastery of lowland Palestine.

ARCHAEOLOGY OF EUROPEANS IN PALESTINE

The archaeological evidence for the expanding role of the Philistines in Palestine has recently been refined. In the intense exchange of people and goods that went on in the eastern Mediterranean, the boundaries between trade, raiding, and piracy were far from rigid. Peoples traveled and cultural artifacts were exchanged throughout the eastern Mediterranean during the late New Kingdom period. However, fortification increased everywhere during the middle and late thirteenth century, an indication that peaceful trade faced increasing hindrances. About 1200 the Mycenaean and Hittite empires collapsed, events associated somehow with the sweep of European rovers and migrants around the eastern coast of the Mediterranean, culminating in the attack on Ramesses III. The organization of power and exchange in the eastern Mediterranean fell apart. Twenty-five years ago, a survey of pottery recovered off the Palestine coast showed almost no southern coastal trade from the twelfth to ninth centuries. With more recent data, that finding must be qualified. Nevertheless, it is still accurate to say that about 1200 B.C.E. import pottery in Palestine virtually ceased.

Archaeologists date the end of the Bronze Age in Palestine technically to the cessation of Mycenaean IIIB and Cypriot pottery imports in Palestine. The latest MycIIIB pottery at Ugarit appeared in a destruction level along with a sword cartouche of Merneptah. At Deir Alla, in the Jordan valley, the latest MycIIIB appeared with a cartouche of Queen Tewosret, the immediate predecessor of Ramesses III. At T. el-Farᶜah in the south coastal plain, the last MycIIIB stage is associated with Tewosret's predecessor Seti II. These correlations point to a date of 1200, give or take a decade. The destruction of Akko also marks the MycIIIB to MycIIIC1b transition. This destruction is not precisely dated, but can be related to the European invasion of the coast about 1190–80 and the beginning of a settled Philistine presence in Palestine. At least one prominent Israeli archaeologist believes that Akko was governed by Sherden during the reign of Ramesses III.

Mycenaean IIIC1b pottery was clearly a feature of a European culture in Palestine during the reign of Ramesses III, lasting to the middle of the twelfth century. It was not, however, the black and red bichrome pottery historians have long called Philistine, which derived from it. Mycenaean IIIC was an Aegean-style successor to MycIIIB made locally rather than imported. It signals the arrival of migrant settlers, Philistines or another European people, in the coastal area, while Ramesses III and the Egyptians were still in control. During this period, lasting Ramesses III's entire thirty-one-year reign, the European migrants adopted elements of Egyptian culture, most noticeably burial in coffins adorned with anthropoid clay masks. The people who used the coffins had become accustomed to using Egyptian scarabs and amulets as well as pottery, perhaps during residence in Egypt itself. These anthropoid coffins were especially popular at Bethshan, where over fifty have been found. Bethshan was a center of Philistine power for two hundred years, until the reign of David.

When so-called Philistine pottery appeared, it was a blend of four ceramic styles: Mycenaean, Cypriot, Egyptian shape and motifs, and Palestinian bichrome technique.[6] Its dominant traits derived from the Mycenaean repertoire and point to an Aegean background. The evidence of many sites, especially Bethshan, T. Seraᶜ, and T. el-Farᶜah south, shows that Philistine pottery could not predate the mid-twelfth century. While some historians hold that MycIIIC ware was manufactured by non-Philistine Europeans and subsequent Philistine ware by an influx of Philistines, most are inclined to believe that Philistine pottery represented only a change in style, not in producing populations. Either way, it is clear that by mid-century the migrant Philistines, after a generation in alliance with and service of the Egyptian occupiers, had adopted Egyptian styles and taken Egypt's place in the culture and politics of Palestine.

The MycIIIC ware was produced all over the eastern Mediterranean, not just in Palestine, in each place locally by newcomers sharing a common Aegean culture.[7] It therefore does not distinguish its producers, Philistines or otherwise, from other groups of European migrants and intruders. It appeared in Palestine in quantity at Ashdod, T. Miqne, T. Safit, probably Gath, and T. Qasile, on the northern border of the main Philistine presence, as far as the Yarkon river. T. Miqne, probably the site of Ekron, covered fifty acres, the largest Iron Age site in Israel. It was surrounded by a mudbrick wall ten feet thick.

Philistine ware appeared in small quantities remarkably suddenly at these sites, in levels containing diminishing quantities of MycIIIC. At both Ashdod and T. Miqne, plain Iron I pottery continued to be used for utilitarian purposes. As at most Philistine sites, Iron I plain ware continued to dominate the ceramic assemblage. Careful note should be taken of this last point, to avoid the mistaken impression that calling a site or its pottery Philistine means that its entire Palestinian populace was abruptly supplanted by an alien race and disappeared without a trace. The Philistines represented a domineering addition to the existing population. With few exceptions, their distinctive ware made up only a small fraction of the pottery of sites where they were located.[8]

Ashdod illustrates the difficulties in interpreting the social significance of Philistine pottery. During the reigns of Ramesses II and Merneptah, Ashdod was a flourishing Palestinian city under Egyptian rule. It has produced many rich Egyptian finds, and quantities of Mycenaean and Cypriot pottery. It was well known to the scribes of Ugarit. About 1200 the city was destroyed, and the imported pottery ceased. The town became smaller, was unfortified, and occupied a different ground plan. The new culture, represented by locally produced MycIIIC pottery, was under strong Aegean influence. Dothan identifies this stratum as a settlement of pre-Philistine rovers. The Philistines themselves are to be located in a further distinguishable stratum dated to the early years of Ramesses III, after the great battle of Ramesses' eighth year. The Philistines located at Ashdod as settlers, not conquerors. The city was replanned and fortified, and lasted until the end of the century.

Mycenaean IIIC ware has been discovered separated from Philistine ware in most Palestinian sites. At T. Mor, an Egyptian fortress that probably served as the port of Ashdod, the pottery included Egypto-Palestinian and MycIIIC; only later did Philistine pottery appear in the mix. At T. Seraᶜ, stratum IX, which dates to Ramesses III, contained no Philistine pottery, only the common Egypto-Palestinian and MycIIIC cultures found all over. In the later stratum VIII, Philistine pottery was plentiful. The Philistine pottery could not be earlier than Ramesses III's twenty-second year, since a bowl inscribed with that date was discovered in stratum IX and there was a gap in occupation between it and stratum VIII. At T. el-Farᶜah south, tombs of Aegean type contained large quantities of thirteenth- and twelfth-century pottery, but no Philistine ware. The cemetery was in active use until at least the time of Ramesses VIII, near the end of the twelfth century. T. el-Farᶜah south became a significant Philistine settlement, but not until the eleventh century, after the end of the Ramesside dynasty. At Lachish, MycIIIB pottery ended with the destruction of the site about mid-twelfth century, marked by a stratum containing a cartouche of Ramesses III and no Philistine pottery. After this destruction, the site remained unoccupied until the tenth century. Neither Lachish nor T. Hesi shows any Philistine pottery. Farther north, Bethshan stratum VI represented the regional headquarters of Ramesses III and shows much MycIIIC but practically no Philistine pottery.

The situation at Dor still farther north should become clear with further excavation. The stratum representing roughly the beginning of the tenth century shows an influx of Cypriot pottery. The earlier strata, however, contain no imported vessels. Too little Philistine ware has so far been discovered to indicate that Dor was a Philistine or Tjeker settlement.

It was thus not the settlement of the Philistines per se, but their interaction with Egyptian and Palestinian culture over a period of time that led to the distinctive pottery style archaeologists label Philistine. The Philistine settlement preceded by a generation the manufacture of Philistine pottery.

The culture of the migrants in Palestine was so similar to that of the thirteenth-century migrant settlements in Cyprus, which historians call Achaean, that the two should probably be regarded as the same. Some have suggested, therefore, that the Philistine migrants to Palestine came most immediately from Cyprus. Their Mycenaean traits show that before settling in Cyprus they came from the Aegean area.

At T. Qasile near the coast, the three strata of Philistine occupation have revealed overlapping temples of increasing size and distinctiveness. The earliest temple plan is similar to one at Hazor, thus imitating local Palestinian practice. As it was enlarged, however, it increasingly resembled shrines in Cyprus, the island of Melos in the Aegean, and Mycenae in Greece. The utensils of the cult show links with Aegean and Cypriot parallels, at the same time Egyptian and Palestinian elements are also evident. In the eleventh century two shrines were built adjacent to each other, for which the only known parallels are to be found again in Cyprus and the Aegean. Similarly, at Joppa the Philistine inhabitants reused a Late Bronze Age temple for their cult.

EUROPEANS TAKE OVER

Egyptian power in Palestine melted away in the second half of the twelfth century. The six generations from then to David saw the development of a Philistine pentapolis, consisting of Gaza, Ashkelon, Ashdod, Gath, and Ekron, as the dominant power in Palestine. Ramesses III had settled the Philistines "in strongholds, bound in my name." Either during his reign or immediately after, the cities that became the pentapolis were probably turned over to the Philistines, who served as administrative and mercenary proxies for the Egyptians, much as Israel served the same purpose farther north. From their coastal and lowland bases, the Philistine lords, known in their own language as *sarns*, encroached on towns and territories they had previously left untouched. For example, five miles east of T. Miqne, biblical Ekron, lies T. Batash, probably biblical Timnah. Whereas MycIIIC pottery is common at Ekron, as mentioned above, excavations at Timnah have turned up no MycIIIC, but much Philistine pottery, indicating that Timnah was taken over by Philistines, probably from Ekron, only after about 1150 B.C.E.

The pentapolis towns had clearly been among the most important of the Egyptian centers. All the Philistine towns show a previous major Egyptian presence except Gath, which has not been sufficiently excavated to decide whether this exception is significant. As the powerful local embodiment of a general European invasion of Syria and Palestine, the Philistines took over the alien if not imperial governing role of the Egyptians. At the same time Ramesses III was expanding Egyptian control into the Shephelah, the Philistines were gaining, or being granted, a foothold in the main coastal and tradeway centers. Ramesses III's struggle with the Philistines led him to support Israel as a counterweight to the Philistines, and this encouraged the continuation of the extension of settlement begun with the fall of Hatti.

The Philistines and other European groups controlled the eastern Mediterranean, but because of their disunity could not take advantage of this control to maintain trade. On land, the Philistines apparently confederated, much as the Israelite chiefs had, and their power soon grew beyond the coast. We have seen their power at Bethshan, and their influence appears in the Jordan valley at many sites and gradually in the highland as well. Philistine land trade may have been instrumental in the rise of the Ammonite state beyond the Jordan east of Jerusalem and Jericho. The Philistines apparently did not have much of a hand in the southern trade into Arabia that grew up during their regime. Philistine pottery has been found at sites such as T. Beit-Mirsim, Bethel, Jerusalem, and T. en-Nasbeh, a few miles north of Jerusalem, in the twelfth century, and many of the other pre-David hill-country sites actually excavated and not just surveyed. The fortress at Gibeah was constructed as a Philistine garrison in the eleventh century. The Europeans' dominance of the Mediterranean was brought to an end when David and the king of Tyre combined to subdue them and restore long-distant trade, which had meanwhile begun to thrive inland, to the Mediterranean.

Pharaoh's court was constrained to make Philistine headmen tax lords in place of Palestinian lords over a large expanse of grain lands, in the two prime breadbaskets of the country, the coastal plain and Jezreel valley. The Philistine plain remained a rich producer of grain. Philistine bullock carts, not widely used in Palestine before the Philistines, facilitated the transport of grain to granaries and the coast. As an alien elite whose land tenure was an extension of Egyptian rule, the Philistines were despised by Palestinians of all classes. Their language and culture were in time submerged beneath the influences of both Egyptian and local culture. Only scattered evidence exists that the Philistines used their own language for some time in Palestine. No supposed Philistine text has yet been deciphered. The identifiable Philistine names are Anatolian in language. The Philistines adopted the Palestinian god Dagon as the god of their chief temple. Dagon was god of grain production, the main source of wealth for these viking lords in Palestine. Like the Vikings in France, the Philistines were soon speaking the main language of Palestine.

The settlement of the Philistines meant an erosion of the power of the Palestinian lords they displaced. The sociopolitical upheaval produced a group of erstwhile Palestinian lords who had no love for the Philistine aliens and were prepared to bide their time until battle could restore their rights to the wealth of the lowlands. Meanwhile, with the dislodging of Egypt and its policy of divide and rule, other areas of settlement and food production were opening up, offering Palestinian lords the opportunity to transfer their control to different parts of the country for the time being.

It is not known for certain that ousted Palestinian lords were to be found among the lords of the new villages, especially those in the highland, which later came under the rule of the king of Israel. The example of Idrimi, however, a fifteenth-century displaced king of a town in Syria, who readily joined a band of *abiru,* confirms what might otherwise be expected, that lowland lords could find a place in the backlands of settlement as well as some distant town, though less likely in the established highland towns such as Shechem, Bethel, Jerusalem, and Hebron. Given the decline in urban life with the decline in Mediterranean trade, the backlands might have been the preferred choice. These urbanites were not peasant farmers, but gangs of fighters accustomed to controlling other people's food production.

In sum, European invaders overran Palestine during the late thirteenth and early twelfth centuries. In the lowland they gradually replaced many of the indigenous elite. Egypt found its bond with Israel all the more important, and encouraged its extension of settlement, which had commenced with the fall of Hatti. When the Egyptian empire collapsed about 1150, the Philistine lords completed their alien takeover of the shrunken New Kingdom colony and set about to complete Egypt's conquest of all Palestine. Within a generation or two of the settlement of the Philistines, the two proxy powers, Israel and Philistia, deprived of their imperial patron but thus released to expand on their own, ended up locked with each other in a struggle for control of the whole territory abandoned by the Egyptian empire in Palestine. At this time, the Assyrian king Tiglath-Pileser I (1115–1077 B.C.E.) subdued Aramean tribes in Syria and campaigned to the Mediterranean, through Amurru, which extended as far south as Byblos and Sidon. From their kings he received gifts. The king of Egypt at the time sent him a gift of a crocodile. Tiglath-Pileser did not interfere in Palestinian affairs. For a brief time, the empires had vacated the Palestinian stage.

During most of the period between Merneptah and Saul, the policy of Israel's chiefs was nominally pro-Egyptian, first as Egyptian allies, then in opposition to the hostile Philistine rulers of the coast and lowlands, who found it increasingly worth their while to attempt to conquer the incipient Israelite kingdoms. From about 1150 to 1000, the basic political pattern in Palestine was the conflict between lowland "Philistines" and highland "Israelites," with some geographical variation. This is the background to the scriptural narratives dealing with Samson and the outlaw David, both Israelite border ruffians who took what advantage they could of divided loyalties.

CHAPTER SIX

The Settlement
of the Highlands

About 1200 B.C.E. Palestine witnessed a reversal of settlement trends. For three hundred years, beginning with the New Kingdom Egyptian occupation of Palestine, settlements had shrunk and receded. Then in the twelfth and eleventh centuries B.C.E., they grew and expanded. Villages began to spread beyond the previous frontiers of settlement, and before long the process accelerated in nearly every section of Palestine. Most of the new settlements were villages or hamlets. There were practically no new towns in the newly settled areas, although during two centuries it is not surprising a few developed. The new settlements were most common in the highland, where they spread from north to south over the course of two hundred harvest seasons, built and inhabited by some eight generations of mixed subsistence dry-farming families.

Some of the newly settled areas became the territory of the chiefdom or kingdom of Israel at the end of the eleventh century, as implied in early biblical texts. Other newly settled areas included northern Galilee, the Negeb, and parts of Transjordan. Many such areas were being settled for the first time since the Middle or Early Bronze Ages.

After this turnaround, settlement and population either held steady or grew for many hundreds of years, until at least the sixth century B.C.E. in most places. Although the expansion of settlement did not produce tribal Israel, it did establish the agricultural base of monarchic Israel. Further growth under the Israelite and Judahite monarchies can be attributed to many factors. The increasing use of iron was particularly important. The apparent reciprocal relationship between the Levant and Greece, whereby one tended to prosper as the other declined, may also have played a role. Thus Mycenaean Greek development reached its pinnacle in the Late Bronze Age while agricultural Palestine stagnated, whereas in the first five centuries of the Iron Age these trends reversed. Central political power played a role.

The subject of the spread of new village settlements in Palestine in the Early Iron Age is usually treated much earlier in works on the origin of Israel. Recent treatments of early Israel, including our own, have tended to equate the village settlement of the highland with the emergence of Israel, implying that one helps to explain the other. The point is sometimes incidental. Finkelstein uses the phrase "Settlement period" for the process of the emergence of Israel mainly because the new settlements are his subject.[1] Nonetheless, the common supposition is that Israel as a distinctive society formed in the highland. The process of escaping to, settling down in, or coalescing in the highland supposedly gave Israel its special character.

Compared with the treatment of early Israel prior to this century, and again prior to the works of Mendenhall, Gottwald, and Chaney, this supposition represented a significant insight. The new highland settlements were connected with early Israel. The settlement in what became Israelite territory was the predominant new settlement—the dog wagging the tail of settlement in other areas. The highland settlement decided the character of tribal Israel for nearly two hundred years.

Nevertheless, the spread of settlement and the origin of Israel were not the same thing. The extent of settlement was not conterminous with Israel, nor Israel with the new settlements. Israel was a tribal force before the reversal of settlement trends, and settlements spread in many areas other than those that became Israelite. Before the spread of villages in the highland, Israelites probably had contacts there, but most Israelites were located elsewhere, in the northern lowlands and outlying settlements. Moreover, there was nothing unique about the spread of settlement that produced highland Israel. Like its people, highland Israelite society was an extension of Palestinian Israel in the thirteenth century. The highland settlement had everything to do with the age-long survival of the name Israel, but nothing to do with its origin.

POLITICAL CHANGE IN THREE STEPS

The extension of settlement into the highland frontier does, however, tell us some things about Israel during this time. Many proposals have been made regarding the historical circumstances that led to the spread of settlement by the indigenous population. These proposals often contain implications for the supposed novel character of the new settlements. They include the fall of the Late Bronze Age empires, the decline in trade, transport, and communication, the depletion of resources in the lowland, grain shortages, population change, a new religious movement, lowland political unrest, peasant revolt, and new technologies. Many complex factors contributed to the change in settlement pattern, and elements of all of these explanations played some role. None, however, has found general agreement as the main reason for the reversal in settlement trends.

The key question to ask about the new settlements is this: what historical change produced the *political* conditions that made living in and farming new areas safe enough for farmers to do it? The spread of settlement and agriculture required order and security, the concurrent spread of protection. Otherwise farmers would have been disinclined to risk farming new areas. Some change in the pattern of rural and frontier political instability to which Israel was already a party activated the spread of settlement. Such a change could be expected to involve or at least significantly affect the dominant tribal entity that was in the area just prior to the spread of settlement and that ended up in control of the majority of new settlements. Since tribal Israel was the political entity in the best position to oversee the spread of settlement and agriculture in the areas that later became highland Israel, the political change must have involved them.

This change was geopolitical, as already indicated at the end of the last chapter. The European invasions of the late thirteenth and early twelfth centuries initiated this change, and it occurred in three stages.

First, the Europeans removed Hatti from the stage. By unraveling frontier politics, this eased the vise that kept Israel's tribal territory squeezed between Hatti and Egypt and triggered the initial spread of tribal control in new frontier settlements. The requisite order and security were provided and maintained by the powerful Israelite tribal confederation created with the Egyptians.

Second, as the Europeans threatened to supplant the Egyptians in Palestine, Ramesses III countered their menace to political equilibrium by bolstering the tribes of

Israel as Egypt's long-standing allies. The ambiguities that had attended this state alliance due to Israel's tribal nature were temporarily resolved. Egypt changed its strategy of impeding the expansion of Israelite territory and instead encouraged Israel's chiefs to oversee the spread of settlement into new lands. This both strengthened the hand of Israel's chiefs and forestalled a European expansion into new lands.

Finally, the Europeans forced Egypt out altogether, took over most of the Palestinian lowland, and sent Palestinian elite clients of the Egyptian occupation packing as well. Many Palestinian lords ended up in Israel's camp. The tribes of Israel, expanding through both accretion and internal growth, dispensed with their Egyptian buttress and emerged in their own right on their new highland agricultural base as the dominant political opposition to the aliens, mostly Philistines, who now ruled lowland Palestine. During the latter part of the twelfth century, a sociopolitical border formed in the Shephelah and elsewhere between the Philistines and Israelites, as the new geopolitical reality in Palestine.

The spread of opportunistic small settlements in areas where settlement had hitherto contracted is a clear indication of both the necessity and the opportunity for the overall village population to produce more grain. Necessity had always been present. It was the opportunity that was distinctive. At this time both necessity and opportunity, push and pull, were affected by the changes in eastern Mediterranean trade and security of travel, transport, and communication, due to the European rovers and their success in wresting control from the Egyptians in the Palestine lowlands. The onslaught of the Europeans weakened Egypt's military and administrative organization. Egypt was forced to accept the addition of a second, overlapping foreign elite and a third, overlapping taxing elite to the agrarian regime.

These developments made village production in the lowlands all the less desirable and manageable. During the first Philistine century, the long arm of the surrogate Philistine regime failed to reach into the marginal areas, where Egypt had discouraged settlement through its divisive tribal policies but where Egypt's control was now fast diminishing. Another wave of Palestinian lords were ousted from their urban positions, and rather than allowing themselves to be deported to Egypt many transferred to the tribal cause, enlarging the ranks of the tribal elite and strengthening the tribes with their fighting skills. When Egyptian strength in the lowland was compromised, whole areas in the highland became available for cultivation.

Under Israelite tribal supervision, the risks of production in the lowlands outweighed those in the sparsely occupied hill country and dry lands. The decentralized organization of tribal control in the marginal areas encouraged new settlements. Once the tide had turned, the tribal elite had the incentive to promote continued extension by relaxing the burden of grain taxes. The tax on labor in tribal territories was obviated. As Hopkins demonstrates, more labor was needed to cultivate more areas. The tribal elite adopted expansionist policies toward their villages in place of Egypt's retractionist policies. But all this came only after the compromising of the Egyptian regime during the first quarter of the twelfth century. Israel's fostering of agricultural expansion did not originate as an isolated policy of Israelite growth, but in reaction to the successive conditions that changed the Israelite tribal elite's relationship to Egypt. Esse's qualification of the notion of a peasant revolt is apt: "Although the lowland population may not have witnessed a peasant revolt in political terms, new opportunities in the hills, combined with a presumably safer environment, may have presented themselves to a population witnessing the fragmentation of Late Bronze Age society,"[2] just as Gottwald and others have argued.

Again, these developments explain not the emergence of Israel, but the change in Israel from a tribal confederation located mainly in northern lowland and frontier Palestine, supported by village agriculture and military subsidies, and tied to Egypt, to a tribal confederation located mainly in the central highlands, still supported by village agriculture, and at first in its fortunes more tied to Egypt, but with the fall of the New Kingdom much less so.

SPREAD OF SETTLEMENTS

Recent archaeological research has greatly clarified the process of settlement in the twelfth and eleventh centuries. The American archaeological approach to the supposed conquest, advanced by Albright and many of his students after the partial excavation of a few large tells, has been decisively invalidated. According to a recent reckoning by Dever, of sixteen sites said by the Bible to have been destroyed during the Israelite invasion, three show archaeological evidence of destruction—the same three today as thirty-five years ago: Bethel, Lachish, and Hazor. (Contrary to Albright, however, the destruction of Lachish is now dated 1175–1150 B.C.E. instead of 1230 B.C.E.) Of the remaining thirteen, seven either were not occupied during the time of settlement or show no trace of destruction. Six remain unexcavated or unlocated. Of thirteen other known sites either not mentioned in the Bible or still unidentified, six were probably destroyed by the

Europeans and one by Merneptah, if he or his army campaigned in Palestine. The other six were destroyed by
uncertain agents, of which accident is the prime suspect.
Dever's conclusion, assented to now by most, is that the
archaeological evidence is overwhelmingly against the
view of an Israelite conquest as presented in the Bible.[3]
The evidence also fails to support the notion of nomadic
infiltration, since there is nothing in the record to indicate
the settlement population was non-Palestinian or, contrary to Finkelstein's latest work, primarily pastoral nomads or seminomads.

Contemporary excavations and especially archaeological surveys have produced a wealth of new information
about the development of highland Israel. Finkelstein's
invaluable book, *The Archaeology of the Israelite Settlement,*
is now the basic source for this development, even though
his conclusion that early Israel represented the sedentari-
zation of a group of seminomads with a tenacious identity
(as assumed by Alt), a group that originated in the West
Bank settlements of the Middle Bronze Age, is improbable. Finkelstein's lucid compendium summarizes the
findings of five major surveys covering western and lower
Galilee, Manasseh, Ephraim, and Judah, in which over
two hundred fifty sites from the early Israelite period were
discovered, and of in-depth excavations at more than
twenty probable early Israelite sites.

Before scanning these surveys, we should note that
although tribes were usually territorial, tribal members
often did not think of themselves primarily in terms of
the territory they occupied or controlled. The tribe's primary identity was in terms of its political organization,
which was variable. As political relationships changed,
so did territorial relationships. The rather definite notions
of tribal territories implied by biblical lists, modern biblical maps, and discussions such as the following are based

on concepts held not by the tribes themselves but by urban courts that preferred not to have to deal with moving targets.

In Finkelstein's analysis, the earliest of the new settlements began in Manasseh, which of the newly settled areas had the largest population at the end of the Late Bronze Age. This northern central highland differed from the highland to the south. It was closer to Israel's earlier traditional sphere of influence, and it possessed relatively wide valleys, only moderately hilly landscape, and the large Shechem basin. These factors encouraged the earliest and densest settlement of all the Israelite areas. The new settlements consisted mainly of unwalled villages and hamlets, covering on average an acre or two. The earlier settlements were along the highland ridge and east of it, in areas immediately suited for growing cereal crops and herding sheep and goats, the activities that continued to provide subsistence for the farmers lorded over by the chiefs of Israel. Only gradually were settlements built up on the slopes to the west, in areas particularly suited to vines and olive orchards, and thus requiring greater stability for continuity of tenure.

By 1988 Zertal's survey of Manasseh had produced a catalogue of one hundred sixty Early Iron Age settlements. Many of the new settlements were located on sites previously occupied during the Middle Bronze Age, more than four hundred years earlier. This was true for example of twelve new villages in the Dothan valley. Excavations at Shechem show continuity between Late Bronze and Early Iron Age settlements, and no destruction or cultural hiatus between the two periods, though archaeologically they are not identical. One unusual site investigated by Zertal centers on an altar, watchtower, or similar construction—its exact nature is still disputed—where two Egyptian scarabs have turned up, one from the thirteenth century B.C.E. and one possibly from the twelfth. The significance of these finds is still unclear, but they show that even in the highland Egyptian ties did not cease with the spread of settlement, for the reasons given above.[4]

From Manasseh the settlements spread into what became the territories of Ephraim and Benjamin, and finally, toward the latter part of the eleventh century, into Judah. In Ephraim only one-quarter of the new sites had been previously occupied. Ephraim is the most thoroughly studied of the new settlement areas, thanks to Finkelstein's timely completion and publication of the Ephraimite survey. Here the contrast between the Late Bronze and Early Iron Age settlement patterns can be described with unusual precision. At first, most villages were located in or near the small valleys that pocket the central range and eastern desert fringe of Ephraimite hills. Settlements appeared also in the western foothills, around Izbet-Sartah. Nearly all these settlements were close to permanent springs, and encountered little resistance from entrenched maquis, much of which had been removed during the Middle Bronze Age. On the broad western slopes of the highland, on the other hand, the abundance of wooded vegetation and paucity of springs hindered immediate settlement. In time, settlers in these areas as well cleared scrub with fire, prepared their fields, and built villages. Here the distance from village to spring tended to be greater than was the case higher up and to the east. The southern slopes, while covering a large area, were the most sparsely settled region of Ephraim because of its aridity and the difficulty of its terrain.

Some settlements terraced nearby hills to increase the surface available for cultivation and to conserve soil and water. However, new terraces were not a factor in making highland settlement possible at this time. In areas such as

the northern slopes where terraces were essential to settlement, they had already been constructed during the
Middle Bronze Age. In areas where they were not essential, including those settled earliest, few terraces were
constructed in the Early Iron Age.

Shiloh was the main Ephraimite settlement. It had been
a major fortified site in the Middle Bronze Age, but with
only a few satellite villages, following the typical Middle
Bronze Age pattern seen also at Shechem, Bethel, Beth-
Zur, and Hebron. Shiloh was destroyed at the beginning
of the New Kingdom occupation of Palestine. Thereafter
it received infrequent visitors, possibly interested, as Finkelstein suggests, in a cult shrine, which remained intact
for about a century before complete abandonment. Shiloh
was resettled in the twelfth century B.C.E. and reached
its height of prosperity in 1100–1050, before Israelite settlement had even begun in many parts of the frontier. Its
importance is shown by the density of villages around it,
two to three times greater than in other parts of Ephraim.
Twenty-two sites were located within six kilometers.
Bethel was surrounded by only twelve villages in a comparable area. It appears that in the Early Iron Age Shiloh
took over Bethel's Late Bronze Age role as the main settlement in this area. There is no reason to doubt that
Bethel was also an early Israelite shrine. However, its
prominence in the Bible stems mainly from the destruction of Shiloh in the middle of the eleventh century, possibly by the Philistines.

Farther south, in Benjamin the Early Iron Age villages
were again founded on the highland ridge and to the east.
The excavation of T. en-Nasbeh in the 1930s provided
the only full plan of a large premonarchic Israelite village,
which was typically elliptical although some of its features
are displayed fragmentarily at other partially excavated
sites. On the western slope were located four "Gibeonite"

towns, which according to early biblical texts were not at first affiliated with Israel. Jerusalem also fell outside Israel's sphere. As Finkelstein points out, none of these five towns had daughter villages; they represented more or less isolated highland political pockets. In Judah, the survey by Ofer found between ten and twelve Early Iron Age sites, most of them north of Hebron. Judah remained on the frontier of settlement during the entire early Israelite period. There were no new towns or villages at all in the Shephelah, which casts doubt upon Albright's identification of T. Beit Mirsim as Israelite.

Finkelstein's figures summarize the highland settlement. In the central hills between the Jezreel valley and the Beersheba valley—most of David's highland Israel—from the Late Bronze Age to the Early Iron Age settlements increased from 30 to 240, an eightfold increase. Of these 240 sites, 96 were in Manasseh, 122 in Ephraim, and 22 in Benjamin and Judah. In addition to these, there were 68 sites in Galilee, 18 in the Jordan valley, and dozens more in Transjordan. The early Israelite population was thus concentrated between Jezreel and Jerusalem. Of the 250 sites in the central highland, 90 percent were in Manasseh or Ephraim. As pointed out, until the end of the eleventh century Judah was only sparsely populated. Only then did numerous settlements appear in Judah and the Beersheba valley. All together more than 350 Early Iron Age sites are known in the newly settled parts of Palestine. These account for four-fifths of all sites thought to have been occupied by Israel during this period.

In Lower Galilee, four Late Bronze Age sites turned into fifteen Early Iron Age sites, as determined by the survey of Gal. In Finkelstein's view, this evidence suggests that the Iron Age settlement of Galilee came late. In the center, Zebulun seems to have been settled no earlier than the late twelfth century B.C.E., and in the east Issachar no earlier than the beginning of the tenth century. Once again, it is important to realize that although the spread in settlement was triggered by specific political changes, the process itself took many generations, during which we know few details of the shifting tribal and lowland politics that determined which areas were settled when.

Upper Galilee was first settled at the end of the twelfth century in a pattern like that in the central highland: small size, more difficult terrain, limited pottery ensemble, and the presence of storage pits. These sites may be identified with biblical Naphtali. Their ceramic culture differed from that of the central highland. The typical collared-rim jar has been found only at the site of the town of Dan. Elsewhere its functions were performed by a distinctive Galilean form of *pithoi,* and in some places a form distinctive of Tyre. At one site, Har Adir, a fortress and remarkable steel axe were uncovered. These probably represent the spread of Phoenician rather than Israelite culture into the highlands.

Excavations at the town sites of Hazor and Dan in the north have particular importance. Hazor was destroyed not long after 1300 B.C.E. and resettled only about 1100, as part of the general settlement of Naphtali. The nearly two-hundred year gap in occupation, during almost the entire period in which Egypt intensified its grip on southern and central Palestine, illustrates the character of this buffer territory as something of a no-man's-land, in which tribal cultivation and herding would have been the main activity. The lack of occupation at nearby Dan between the Middle Bronze Age and the twelfth century confirms this picture. The new settlements at both Hazor and Dan were modest, with storage pits and, in the case of Dan, Tyrian *pithoi* as well as *pithoi* of a type similar to collared-rim jars.

Elsewhere in greater Palestine, settlement was expanding in a similar way. In Gilead and the major settlement areas of Transjordan, identified even then as Ammon, Moab, and Edom, where islands of greater rainfall attracted agriculture, villages advanced in the same process of tribally supervised settlement and agriculture. Most of these tribes, however, were more or less independent of Israel, until the house of David conquered their territories in the tenth century. They did not themselves develop into states until later, and in the case of Edom not until the Neo-Assyrian period, as proposed by Knauf.

When the spread of settlement began in the twelfth century, the new villages were sometimes located near major towns. This was the case near Dothan and Shechem in Manasseh. It has been shown on the basis of settlement patterning that even in the Middle Bronze Age many highland villages—though not all—were not under urban dominance. This feature of Palestinian village culture helps to explain how Israelite villages could develop for as long as they did unattached or dominated by urban sites that in some cases were close by. The hostile border between the Philistine and Israelite territories, however, developed its own character. As the animosity between the two confederations grew, the border between them became less safe for farming, and was left unsettled. Only heroic ruffians such as Samson could span such a border with impunity, and, as hinted by the biblical narrative, in time the tribe of Dan was forced to migrate from the foothill border zone north into Tyrian territory in search of more secure conditions.

Finkelstein estimates the highland population west of the Jordan in the mid-twelfth century was about twenty thousand. The fighting force that could be raised from such an aggregate was not large, especially considering its probable disunity. A century later, on the eve of the transition to monarchy, the numbers were perhaps double that. Only Manasseh and eastern Ephraim were densely settled; settlement in the other Israelite territories was sparse. It is not clear that the change in settlement led at first to an increase in population. Probably people simply relocated for the first generation or two. Some early settlements may have begun as Alt and his students imagined, as enlarged highland shielings for herders who resided in the lowland during the growing season. In Knauf's view, prior to the spread of settlements there were only small groups of unorganized pastoralists in the highland, much as in Oman in more recent times. Fritz suggests that during much of the settlement period, villages would occupy a given site for only a generation or two and then move to a new site after the soil was depleted. This may well describe the constant opening up of new fields for cultivation, if not the routine abandonment and rebuilding of stonebuilt villages and homesteads. (In any case, the contrast with settlement stability in the monarchic period is marked.) Then later, in the eleventh century, a great increase in population occurred under the productive conditions of the highlands and tribal control.

ARCHAEOLOGY OF VILLAGES

About twenty Early Iron Age highland villages have been excavated in whole or part, so that their character and something of the lives of their inhabitants can be known. The evidence shows just what would be expected: the transfer of subsistence farming from the lowland frontier to the highland frontier. People who subsisted on dry farming in the lowlands moved to the highlands and did the same thing. Moreover, these village communities show cultural continuity with the lowlands, except in areas of adaptation to highland conditions. Among the

sites excavated are Ai and Raddana in Ephraim. At Ai
about twenty houses were excavated, out of an estimated
forty. The population was estimated at between 150 and
300. The village covered under three acres, less than one-
tenth the size of the Early Bronze Age city that had occupied the same site over a thousand years earlier. A few
miles to the west, Raddana appears to have covered
roughly the same area as Ai, but only six houses were
excavated there, with room for thirty to forty individuals.
The whole population apparently numbered under a hundred. Raddana may have begun as an early Israelite ham-
let. The evidence of its foundation is ambiguous. A brief
alphabetic inscription was found on a jar handle dating
to the late thirteenth century B.C.E. A certain krater from
Raddana seems to show affinities with a Hittite style.
These suggest a date prior to the major phase of settlement
expansion. On the other hand, several metal objects were
found, including an iron plow tip, and the developed
pillared houses at the site suggest a later date.

Not all new Early Iron Age settlements can be unmis-
takably associated with the extension of Israelite control
over frontier agriculture. Giloh in the hills south of Jerusalem represents a tiny hilltop site fortified in 1200 B.C.E.
Its pottery shows clear Iron I elements, but there is nothing to indicate it was not a lowland Palestinian outpost
from the coast, rather than a shieling or incipient agricultural settlement. Izbet Sartah, excavated by Finkelstein, is another example. Finkelstein assumes it was
settled from the east, but there is no clear indication of
such a migration. Its pottery was nearly identical with
that of nearby Gezer, which was not an Israelite settlement
in the twelfth and eleventh centuries. Such sites near coastal control are particularly difficult to assess. In the hills
of southern Judah, T. Halif and T. Beit Mirsim, across
the valley from each other, were occupied alternately for

hundreds of years. Then just before 1200 both were settled at the same time. Taanak, in the Jezreel valley just south of Megiddo, quite a large settlement in the early part of the Late Bronze Age, was reduced in size by the end of the period. In approximately 1200 it was the site of considerable new occupation. An isolated cuneiform tablet at Taanak, possibly from an early twelfth-century context, registers the receipt of a shipment of grain in a style associated with an occupying state, not tribal administration. Recent work by Greenberg has correctly removed T. Beit Mirsim from the discussion of early Israel altogether.

The continued direct contact with the state is also illustrated by the main new settlement in the Negeb, T. Masos, seven miles east of Beersheba. The excavators assumed T. Masos was an Israelite settlement, but serious doubt has been cast on this assumption by Mazar and Finkelstein. Mazar suggests T. Masos represents the extension of coastal influence, especially Philistine, into the Negeb. The lowest three Iron Age strata are of primary interest. The oldest settlement, during the first half of the twelfth century, left only ash pits, grain pits, and beaten earth floors. Its pottery was Palestinian, with no Philistine examples. A scarab of Pharaoh Seti II (about 1198–1192) appeared here. In the next stratum, built about 1150, a pillared house appeared, along with what the excavators thought was a governmental structure of some kind. The third stratum covered from twelve to fifteen acres and featured public buildings and an entire array of pillared houses. These give evidence of Egyptian and coastal Palestinian influences. Philistine and Midianite pottery was found, in addition to coastal pottery forms and a valuable carved ivory lion's head. This third phase represented the greatest development of T. Masos. It lasted a century or more, from the end of the twelfth century. Thus during its heyday T. Masos was three times larger than the largest new highland village site, and more than ten times larger than other Early Iron Age sites in the Negeb. T. Masos was at its height before any Israelite thought of settling in Judah, so it is quite separated from the main Israelite area. The public buildings, coastal architectural and ceramic influences, and the scattered finds all diverge from the typical Israelite pattern.

It is thus clear that the territories later identified with the tribes of Israel were settled in diverse times by diverse groups. Whatever coherence the tribal coalition called Israel in the thirteenth century possessed, it was greatly attenuated during the period of settlement extension. Meyers's topological appraisal of the Galilean tribes has shown that their territories were not based on geographical or ecological factors, but on political factors, especially the need to organize militarily to repulse damaging trooper raids from the lowlands and bandit raids by other tribesmen. This suggests a tribal political coherence and significance that was greater at the level of the named tribes than at the level of Israel, which fits the likelihood that Israel continued to be predominately an elite organization and concept. As mentioned, tribes also migrated to avoid conflict.

One indication of the secondary nature of tribal groups in the territories settled later in the period is the tendency for their names to refer to geographical features: Judah, Asher, Naphtali, and Zebulun ("highland") probably take this form, and Benjamin means the "southern" tribe, presumably in relation to the northern focus of early Israel, or to Manasseh and Ephraim. The notion of Israelite ethnicity is no more necessitated by tribal organization than by state rule, under which historians have wrongly supposed it was reinforced or supplanted by an Israelite nationalism. Unless appropriately qualified, notions of ethnicity and nationalism are quite out of place in the discussion of ancient Palestinian society.

ISRAEL NOT ARCHAEOLOGICALLY DISTINCTIVE

Important features marked highland tribal village culture during the period of settlement extension. These included the small agricultural-pastoral village and its form; the pillared house, which became popular in the Early Iron Age and continued as the dominant house type in monarchic Israel; the profusion of pits for local storage; and the modest repertoire of pottery types, dominated by basic cooking pots and large storage jars, particularly the collared-rim jar. Not surprisingly, these features do not distinguish Israelite from non-Israelite sites in greater Palestine, since Israel was primarily a political and not a cultural identification. There exists no cultural artifact that is a consistent indicator of the presence of Israelites. Together these features merely characterize most of the villages of the newly cultivated areas that were probably founded and developed mostly under tribal authority, regardless of whether or to what degree such authority was Israelite. They do, therefore, characterize in general the settlers and their settlements who worked the main new land base of political Israel during the twelfth and eleventh centuries.

Village Form. The new highland villages were designed for the cultivation of arable and, to a lesser extent, orchards, and for the keeping of livestock. Their plans were often oval or elliptical, with housing surrounding a central pen area for livestock and blocking off easy access and escape by livestock.

Pillared House. The pillared house (or "four-room" house) likewise fulfilled the needs of the relatively prosperous farming family. The typical village house with stone foundations and probably stone upper walls was a small rectangular building constructed out of the ubiquitous limestone of the highland. The entrance was located at one of the narrow ends, off an exterior courtyard. Upon entering the house, to the right or left one would find a row of piers, or pillars, typically four in number but sometimes less, arranged from front to back for nearly the length of the house. These pillars defined a set of animal stalls, easily accessible from the house entrance. The pillars were frequently joined with a low, thin curtain wall, which sometimes included a built-in trough. At Ai, and thus probably elsewhere, these side stables were sometimes entered through arched passages about two and one-half feet high, suitable for animals but not people. The livestock were kept in these pillared stalls and could feed at the troughs. Opposite the stalls, along the other long wall, was a rectangular room, occasionally divided in two, and along the back wall, stretching the entire width of the house, another room, with its entrance almost always in the middle, directly opposite the entrance to the house. The main room or vestibule usually had a hearth, oven, and sometimes cisterns. The side stables never had these. The floor of the main room was often plastered. The stables were typically paved with stones.

The four "rooms" for which the house was previously named were thus the long vestibule or inner court, the set of stalls to one side, the long room (or two) to the other side, and the broad room to the back. The walls and pillars carried an upper story, however, which was probably walled off as part of the dwelling. In this way the house could have had altogether as many as eight rooms. At Ai, ceiling beams were just over five feet off the floor. In the Negev, on the other hand, beams could measure more than six feet off the floor. The pillared house was no hovel. Though far from spacious, it was a well-constructed, multipurpose dwelling of sizable proportions, for housing families that by peasant village standards could be quite large.

It was pointed out by Shiloh that ninety-five percent of the pillared houses known in Palestine occur in settlements that have some chance of being Israelite. He thus preferred to label them as Israelite in type. Perhaps 10 out of 150 examples appear elsewhere. However, there is a lessening propensity to beg the question of the nature of early Israel by implying that Israel was a cultural or ethnic designation. Some scholars continue to believe that the typical village plan and pillared house layout originated with the nomadic tent settlement and tent design. This idea also is now less widely held. It is based on the view that presettlement Israel consisted mostly of pastoral nomads, an increasingly problematic view for which there is little archaeological evidence. The forms of settlement and individual dwelling can be explained from functional requirements of rural village production, without reference to the long-term background of the settlers. Furthermore, since the pillared house appeared for the first time in the twelfth century B.C.E., with only certain Egyptian house features as possible antecedents, there is no reason to wonder where the settlers got their new housing ideas any more than their new building skills. Both lay quite within the capabilities of the lowland farming class, tribal or otherwise, of the thirteenth century and earlier.

Grain Pits.   The third noteworthy feature of the highland villages was the grain storage pit. The proliferation of such pits during the settlement period contrasts sharply with their near absence before and after. They appear in great numbers all over excavated village sites, both inside and outside the houses. Such installations were typical of small-scale rural production. They demonstrate more clearly than any other feature the decentralized nature of highland production during the settlement period, in contrast to the centralized production and storage facilities, including silos and storehouses, implied for the earlier Egyptian period in the lowland and characteristic of the later period of the monarchy in the highland. Similar pits are found in every archaeological period in Palestine, but their numbers vary greatly from period to period. The Early Iron Age was a period in which they proliferated.

The pits were shaped either like a bell or a bottle. They could be large, up to ten feet wide and sixteen feet deep. The pits were lined with a variety of substances, including stone, lime plaster, and ash, all found in excavation. Ethnographic parallels suggest that clay and dung could also have been used. Some of the pits were used as cisterns. These were usually plastered, but some found were not. Recently researchers for the Lahav Grain Storage Project demonstrated exactly how most of these pits were used for grain storage. They stored grain in similar pits for four to six months. This experiment showed that pit storage protected the grain from rats and mice, dampness, and bacteria. The main problem the pits did not entirely solve was insects.

Pottery Types.   Finally, the assemblage of pottery types in highland villages was typically modest. The commonest articles were simple cooking pots and large storage jars. The collar-rimmed storage jar was modeled on large *pithoi* used in the highland during the Middle Bronze Age. In the Early Iron Age it appeared mainly in the central highland, where it can account for as much as one-third of the pottery at a typical site. It was also found in Transjordan in roughly the same numbers, and in the coastal plain and northern valleys in far fewer numbers. It does not appear north of the Jezreel valley except at Dan, although similar forms of storage jars do appear, including Tyrian *pithoi*. The collar-rimmed jar is thus not an indicator of Israelite settlements.

The distribution of the large storage jar shows that it was used for the local communal storage of fluids produced in the vine and orchard areas of new settlement—wine and oil—and for water. The jar appeared with the beginning of the spread of settlement. It went out of use during the tenth century, as under the new monarchies wine and oil were increasingly produced for the state and for export rather than local consumption. At that time the transport and export of wine and oil required smaller containers.

In sum, the distinctive features of the new settlements relate to the production of food and to the relative security of efficient housing and the decentralized retention and storage of food, all in a political environment that, while not without its hazards, hardships, and injustices, did not entail the stunting prey on production by urban elites. The discovery of a bronze bull figurine seven inches long and five inches high at an apparently twelfth-century rural shrine in Manasseh may hint at the veneration of El, which must be assumed was a part of Israelite tribal culture. The Manasseh bull is similar to a Late Bronze Age bull figurine found at Hazor. It is probable that Shiloh served as the main shrine of Ephraim during its period of prosperity. Whether the tribes of Israel adhered to a central shrine during the diverse stages of highland and other frontier settlement is dubious. The cults of the highland were presumably as decentralized as its economy, although the chiefs may have had preferred localities where they gathered.

ISRAEL VERSUS EUROPEANS

Politically the highland inhabitants belonged to tribal village groups, since no new towns were created or settled in the highlands during this period. The old sites of Shechem, Bethel, and Jerusalem were inhabited, but they did not grow and for several generations did not exercise typical control over the extensive agricultural countryside, as at least Shechem and Bethel had done in the Late Bronze Age. Shechem became virtually deserted during the latter half of the settlement period, 1125–1000. Palaces, site walls, and public storehouses were entirely absent from the new settlements in the beginning and at most sites for the entire settlement period. They simply did not form a part of the culture of the new settlements. The tribal character of early Israel was thus maintained. This was made possible partly by the widespread disruption of political and trade alignments in the Early Iron Age, which, quite apart from Palestinian hostility toward the Europeans, limited the incentive among highland chiefs for urban-style control over the highland's agricultural production.

Given the defined areas first settled by Israelite tribes, the tribal cohesion of the New Kingdom period persisted during the rest of the twelfth and eleventh centuries. About the middle of the twelfth century, the two great surrogate powers in Palestine, the Philistine oligarchy and the chiefs of the tribes of Israel, came into their own. As holders of the lowland arable with access to lowland military tactics, the Philistines were more powerful in the main grain growing areas of Palestine. Moreover, unlike Egypt they lacked a long-standing relationship with the local tribes, and they felt no need for such a relationship. They could assume that it was only a matter of time before at least one of them would conquer the settled highlands.

They pressured the chiefs of Israel, found increasingly in the highland as well as lowland, compelling them to promote further settlement in other areas, and fostered the extension of settlement in their own areas of control at the same time. Many villagers under Israel moved into the hills, gradually, over a period of a hundred years, to take advantage of the more favorable political circumstances maintained for the time being by the chiefs of Israel.

Before long, the Israelite tribes of the twelfth and eleventh centuries became predominantly a highland tribal society. As intimated at the end of the last chapter, the basic political pattern in Palestine during the latter part of the settlement period consisted of standoffs between highland and lowland, which was nearly, though not completely, the same as between the chiefs of Israel and the oligarchs of the European controlled lowland cities. As more Palestinian groups who did not inhabit the highlands, such as the tribes of Simeon and Asher, affiliated with Israel, and territories other than the central highlands were opened to settlement, the match between Israel and the highlands became less obvious. By this time, however, Israel's elite were already on the way to developing a confederated identity based almost exclusively on opposition to the European aliens.

The sociopolitical consolidation of Israelite identity is illustrated archaeologically by the animal bones found in the excavation of T. Miqne, biblical Ekron, at the foot of the Shephelah near where one of the main passes into the highland emerges on the coastal plain. At Ekron, under Philistine rule pigs and cattle became more prevalent in the economy, supplanting sheep and especially goats. The species favored indicate an intensification of production, especially of cereals, in one of the great breadbaskets of lowland Palestine. They also indicate less economic and social interaction with highland pastoral production. The destruction of Lachish in 1175–1150 B.C.E. may have been a prelude to the development of this cultural barrier. Likewise, Finkelstein interprets the abandonment of Izbet-Sartah early in the eleventh century as a sign of the warming up of hostilities between the lowland and highland.

The highland settlers' aversion to the Philistines, for both political and cultural reasons, continued to foster a quasi-united front in opposition. Through this opposition, the Philistine oligarchy replaced the Egyptian pharaoh as the focus and foil for the tribal political coherence termed Israel. Hopkins has proposed in addition that the shift in settlement to the highland produced a shortage of labor, and that the social ties established in the process of meeting this shortage communally was a bonding element in Israelite social formation.

Israel's political coherence at the tribal elite level and its attendant intensification are illustrated in the archaeological record in the pattern of settlement in Ephraim by the end of the eleventh century. If the settlements are divided into large sites and small sites, in each topographical region of Ephraim the large sites were evenly spaced in relation to one another. In the northern central range, for example, where the heaviest population concentrated, there was only one large site in each valley. Then in many cases there were a few small villages and sites with just a few houses near the large village. This pattern witnesses to the social stratification of the highland.

The Philistine lords mainly attacked the highland settlements not through the southern slopes of the highland, but through the more approachable middle and north. Political turmoil flared in many localities. In Ephraim, by the middle of the eleventh century, the villages of Raddana and Ai ceased to exist, and the great village of Shiloh was destroyed. As indicated most recently by Finkelstein, it was at this time, in the second half of the eleventh century, that Philistine pottery began to appear in quantity in the highland. As mentioned previously, it has turned up at T. en-Nasbeh, Bethel, and other sites, including T. Aitun, Beth-Zur, Jerusalem, T. el-Ful, Raddana, and Ai.

Despite the supposed role of the Philistines in the destruction of Shiloh, no Philistine pottery has yet been discovered anywhere in Ephraim. Still, the Philistines were gaining the upper hand, as expected. Within two generations, however, all Palestine was under the nominal kingship of an Israelite rather than Philistine, the result of circumstances that led directly to the beginning of the Hebrew Scriptures and the traditional interpretations of Israel's origin.

CHAPTER SEVEN

The Evidence
of the Scriptures

The Hebrew Scriptures, whose formation as such began
in the tenth century B.C.E., ostensibly say a great deal
about early Israel. Although the Scriptures do not contain
a historical account of Israel's origin and early history,
they reveal much about Israel during the century or so
prior to David. Some of the earliest Scriptures refer often
to the Israel of that time, and a few of the apparently
archaic texts in the Scriptures were composed or written
at that time. However, the earliest Scriptures reveal even
more about the circumstances surrounding the beginning
of the Hebrew Scriptures.

The purpose of this chapter is not to mention everything the Scriptures tell us about Israel before David,
which includes much detail even if it is often difficult to
assess. The most important information, the numerous
indications of the tribal nature of early Israel and the hints
of Egyptian partnership, has already played its essential
role in our understanding of Israel's origin. Instead, this
chapter will provide a brief look at the transformation of
Israel into the state organization that produced much of

the Bible, the beginnings of the state Scriptures, some particular texts that predate the state and what they suggest about the political circumstances of eleventh century Israel, and the origin of the portrayals of early Israel promulgated in the state Scriptures. It is necessary, after all, to have a concept, consistent with the history of early Israel, of the source that poses the question of the historical origin of Israel in the first place, but which gives such incomplete answers. Thus the subject of this chapter is not the origin of Israel, but the origin of what the Hebrew Scriptures say about the origin of Israel.[1]

TRIBAL MONARCHY

After a century of rule in the lowlands, the Philistine lords had taken hold of the network of land routes not only along the coast and up to the region of Hazor, but also in the Jordan valley and the Transjordan plateau. No doubt plagued by internal struggles, nevertheless they were doggedly positioning themselves to re-create the New Kingdom in Palestine, if not as a unified monarchy. Their bronze work reached new hardness with an increased tin component. They were the first people in Palestine to make extensive use of iron in warfare. With hard metal weapons and tactics for hill country fighting developed in their homelands and in roving, they campaigned deeper into the hills against the highland Israelites. The goal of the Philistine battalion in the hill country was to seize the ridge route and at least one cross route to the northern end of the Dead Sea, and to subdue the Israelites in the process. They defeated Israelite warriors at Ebenezer in the coastal foothills of Ephraim, at or not far from the early settlement of Izbet-Sartah, and apparently sacked Shiloh, in the heart of Israelite territory, about 1050 B.C.E. Both battles left their sting throbbing in the Bible. The Philistines established garrisons in several localities deep in the hills, including at Gibeah in the heartland of Benjamin, and made plans to join up with Ammonite chiefs to the east. At this point they seemed well on their way to achieving their goal, and Egypt could do nothing to stop them.

As the Philistine domination of Palestine progressed, the Israelite tribal elite functioned increasingly as a ruling class. Given their need to encourage the rationalization of both valuable labor and the intensification of agriculture, the aforementioned hierarchical partitioning of tribal society took its expected course.[2]

The chiefs' efforts to assert tribal rule against Philistine state rule did not unite the highland peasantry. In the highlands, which were fast resuming their role as an extension of developments in the lowland, no one had an effective interest in promoting cultural or political homogeneity at the lower end of the social scale. This was typical and expected. Even when people in a given area start from the same cultural and linguistic baseline—which was not the case in the highland—a cultural drift immediately sets in and spreads them apart. The previously discussed bases for a villager's identity, such as caste, clan, village, and cult, scarcely overlapped. A villager's political identity was also variable, depending on the fortunes of patrons.

By the end of the eleventh century, one of the highland chiefs, not of the largely deserted town of Shechem, had assumed the prerogative of royal sovereignty, which meant taking command in battle and investing himself with the right, which in theory was absolute, to assign fiefs to retainers and tax the entire produce of a claimed territory. The Bible presents Saul as the first Israelite king. This picture comes from documents written to defend David's usurpation, fault David's opponents, and sanction the political role of Israelite local saints such as Samuel. There may have been earlier Israelite "kings" whose names are not preserved because Saul's court produced few if any documents. Saul's father Kish was a wealthy Benjaminite, who had a particular stake in stopping the Philistines from closing the coast-to-Jordan trail through the Israelite highland and expanding north and south from there. His son commanded the willing Israelite forces against the lowland invaders.

It should come as no surprise that the tribal organization was now headed by a king. Recently some historians have been inclined to refer to Saul as a chieftain rather than a king. There may be some wisdom in this. However, recall that tribes and their elites did not simply coexist with urban domination and state rule, but were an integral part of such rule. "Tribes or tribal confederations were identified throughout history with the formation of dynasties and contributed to the military and administrative cadres of a number of states. The importance of the tribal idiom in recruiting, mobilizing, and organizing people has varied historically and according to circumstances. But the tribe has always been a potent political force."[3]

Saul captured Gibeah from the Philistines and set up court there. He defeated the Philistines just to the east, in the pass of Michmash. With a hold on the eastern slopes, he crossed the Jordan and at Jabesh-Gilead pushed the Ammonite army south out of Gilead. Saul thus came close to expelling the Philistines and their allies from the Jordan valley and driving them back through the Jezreel valley to the coast.

The Philistines, organized in the erstwhile Egyptian strongholds in the Aegean pattern of an oligarchic confederacy of palace cities, coalesced to fight back. Saul pressed his recent advantage north into the lowlands, where the Jordan and Jezreel valleys met, attempting to capture a position across the great tradeway to Damascus and the north. The decisive battle was joined near the Philistine stronghold of Bethshan, at Mount Gilboa. The Philistines routed the Israelites. Saul and three of his four sons lost their lives. The fortunes of the house of Saul had suffered a calamitous reversal, and a Philistine victory throughout Palestine loomed. There was little left to stop them now.

The areas of Palestine remaining outside of Philistine control fell under the rule of two parties, the fourth son of Saul, Ishbaal, in the north over Israel, and a one-time Judahite retainer of Saul and brigand vassal to the Philistines named David in the south, together with their respective followings. Ishbaal's name, formed with Baal rather than Yahweh, may be another indication of the highland chiefs' increasing reintegration into lowland political and economic patterns. Mazar has noted signs of Baal worship in Early Iron Age highland cult centers with names such as Baal-perazim, Baal-hazor, and Baal-shalishah. Rosen has added Baal-judah and possibly Baal-tamar to the list.[4]

Saul's cousin and militia commander Abner arranged to have Ishbaal confirmed as king in Mahanaim over parts of Gilead, Geshur to the east of the Sea of Galilee, an eastern section of the Jezreel valley, Ephraim, and the Kishite heartland of Benjamin, all areas that the Philistines had not yet conquered. As often occurred in the subsequent three centuries of kingship in Israel (in contrast to Judah), the general of the army, in this case Abner, was de facto ruler, in a position to divert or usurp the kingship.

DAVID FULFILLS THE EUROPEAN DREAM

David of Judah was a young son of a wealthy family of Bethlehem, the house of Jesse, in the service of Saul. As the youngest of seven or eight sons, David could expect no favor or inheritance and hence sought a career in the king's entourage, as a harpist and fighter. A skilled combatant and aggressive opportunist, he became a battalion commander and married the king's daughter Michal. David's ambition led to rivalry with his lord and patron, who in time ousted him from his court. He fled beyond the king's reach to the wilderness of Judah to the east and south and gathered about him an outlaw band. He sustained his gang through thieving, mercenary work, extortion, and protection. He carried on with no known assistance from his brothers, though sons of both brothers and sisters joined him. His nephews Joab, Abishai, and Asahel, all sons of his sister Zeruiah, played an important role. Joab was his army commander, Abishai chief of his bodyguard, and Asahel his hit man, later held accountable for the deaths of Abner and Amasa, another nephew. Though these sons of Zeruiah held important positions, in the end David used them as scapegoats for despicable deeds for which he could be charged. Although David was temporarily deprived of his wife Michal, he was able to appropriate Saul's wife Ahinoam as his own. Saul's former wife bore David's first son. David aimed to seize the throne of Israel if he could.

As David's power on the margins of Judah grew, he expanded his influence in its heartland. The chief family was the clan of Caleb, who resided in and around the main town of Hebron. A wealthy Calebite named Yether had married a daughter of Jesse, Abigail, thus becoming a brother-in-law to David. On the pretext that Yether had spurned David's protection racket, David ordered him murdered and married Abigail himself—a violation of incest taboos, but a known practice among ancient royalty and quite within the scope of a man of David's arrogance. His sister Abigail became the mother of his second son.

He now had a private army, marriage ties with the dominant families of both Israel (the house of Saul) and Judah (the house of Caleb), and as a wealthy landholder by marriage a substantial foothold in the growing mixed economy of his newly settled homeland.

As the territory under David's control expanded into the lowland, his tangles with the European lords of the lowland became more frequent. Interested in more than winning skirmishes against a superior foe on its own turf, he joined forces with the Philistines as vassal to Achish, the king of Gath, who was glad to corral the mischievous guerrilla and his fighters. Achish set him up as landlord in Ziklag to the south of Gath, where David was able to provide his troops with not only more plunder but also the steady income of produce taxed from the peasants of Ziklag. David performed useful service for his Philistine master, including pressing into the desert against such pastoral tribes as the Amalekites, whom he reportedly decimated.

To all intents and purposes, David had become the equivalent of a powerful Negeb tribal sheikh, with an urban base but extensive control over marginal and uncultivated lands and the trade route to the southwest and southeast. David's redistribution of booty not only enriched his own band, but also reached homeward into the Judahite hills, where he sent gifts to potential backers in Hebron and most of the important villages. His power over the region spiralled upward: as his storehouse and gifts grew, so the number of those dependent on him and thus willing to follow him and fight for him grew, helping him in turn to increase his storehouse. After two years David abandoned his service in Ziklag and returned to the hills. With him went a force of European mercenaries, the Cerethites, Pelethites, and probably Carians, and Ittai of Gath, a Hittite or Hurrian mercenary, with his troop of some six hundred men.

David took Hebron, apparently with little struggle, having achieved what Saul had failed to do. For himself he added well-armed mercenaries to his guerrilla force; for the Judahites he checked the Philistine advance. In Hebron he claimed kingship of Judah, in title and prerogatives. Like it or not, Judah now had what Israel lacked, a sovereign with his own private military, supported outside the heartland, who could keep Philistines at bay—but only with European fighters of his own. His strategy had been less to beat the Europeans than to join them, and his victory over Judah and Israel using European forces completed in fact if not in name the Philistine conquest of the highland. The basis for a regional kingdom was thereby laid by an Israelite, and the lowland harassment of the highland was thus transformed, legalized, and in time organized into sweeping class-based exploitation.

David sent agents north to Geshur and Jabesh-Gilead. He took in marriage a royal daughter of Geshur, Maacah, who bore his third son, Abishalom (Absalom). Ishbaal deemed these diplomatic overtures a violation of sovereignty. A force under Abner met a force under David's generals near Gibeon. Abner was decisively defeated, putting the rule of Benjamin in doubt. Before long Abner was prepared to transfer his own and his Benjaminite bondsmen's allegiance to David. David pressed his claim to the daughter of Saul, Michal, whom Ishbaal turned over in a last attempt to forestall the usurper. Abner transferred to David's side, but soon afterward ended up murdered by David's nephew.

Only Ishbaal stood in the way of David's clenching the monarchic title of Israel. Recognizing the inevitable, two

Benjaminite retainers assassinated their king in Mahanaim. They expected David's approval, but David astutely condemned their work and had them publicly executed. Having made himself the dominant power in the hill country, confirmed his role as close ally and confidant of Jonathan, Saul's son, reestablished his status as son-in-law of Saul, ordered, in all likelihood, the murder of Israel's commander, and possibly their king as well, and striven to acquit himself of all wrongdoing toward the house of Saul, David succeeded to the rule of Israel. The Israelite sheikhs journeyed to Hebron to pledge their loyalty to David, who, having supplanted Saul and Ishbaal as king of Israel, combined in his person the rule of the two highland kingdoms. Not having risen to power through the tribal network, David now undertook to co-opt the tribes' identities in an attempt to neutralize latent tribal resistance to his monarchy.

In Hebron David had three more sons by three more wives. He apparently set up trade relations with Tyre involving wool, an essential product of his area of rule, and other products. The remains of palaces and granaries discovered at Lachish and Bethshemesh indicate he districted Judah during his reign in Hebron along lines other than tribal. Seven years after taking Hebron and two years after the death of Saul, with Ishbaal dead and Israel handed over to him, David captured Jerusalem with his own force and moved his capital there. It became his own city, the "City of David," a neutral and strategic locality on the border between his united kingdoms.

At this time, apparently, David ousted the Philistines, again opposed to him, from the Valley of Rephaim, which led down from the highland ridge to the lowland through a depression between the two kingdoms. The *rephaim* for which the valley was named were deceased local military heroes (in the Greek sense of "departed greats") whose divine patron was the god Rapha (possibly an epithet of El, as in Rapha-el). An archival fragment from David's court relates how his fighters held the Philistines back by beating their best candidates for hero status, stout members of the military sodality called votaries of Rapha. One of them, Dodo, captured David and was about to kill him, but instead was done in by Abishai. Dodo and his father Joash had Semitic names: he was a Palestinian knight fighting for the Philistines. The political division between lowland and highland had a significant ideological element, and by David's time individuals and gangs had no more difficulty than David himself crossing the boundary in both directions to fight on the other side. Among David's Palestinian fighters, Sibbecai, from near Bethlehem, killed the votary Saph, Elhanan from Bethlehem killed the votary Goliath (a deed later attributed to David), and Jonathan, a nephew of David and hence also from Bethlehem, killed a nameless votary remembered for having six fingers and six toes.

Three centuries before David, Jerusalem had been one of three or four small towns in the mountains of Palestine whose rulers controlled only small sections of a largely unsettled region. Though still small, Jerusalem was now the capital of an expanding empire centered in a highland more densely settled and farmed than at any previous time in its history. David had captured the kingdoms of the highlands through fighting, opportunism, gathering strength on the margins of the kingdoms, deft patronage of Judahite disaffected at all levels of the social scale, and, most important, allying himself with Europeans. From his highland political base, he expanded his dominion by increments until he controlled nearly the whole of Palestine from the Red Sea to the northern Biqa valley, in Lebanon.

In the highland, David imposed his energetic royal command on what was still a largely tribally organized society. He was never popular in the modern sense. The basis of what loyalty he enjoyed was the expansion of his kingdoms through conquest. His domination of the tribes of Edom and Moab was an extension of his control over the Judahite drylands and Negeb. He defeated the Moabites in battle and executed two-thirds of his prisoners of war. He was allied with the king of the tribes of Ammon, whose father had supported him, probably as just one more "Philistine," against Saul. For the Ammonites, the threat of Saul evaporated and the threat of David took its place. Ammon appealed to the Aramean king Hadadezer, who like David ruled a united kingdom, Zobah and Bethrehob. Against their coalition David won three battles, at Rabbah, in the northern Transjordan, and near Damascus, and took over the extensive Aramean lands of the northeast. Along the coast he defeated resisting Philistine elements and negotiated an alliance with Tyre. Everywhere he reigned he placed loyal troops in garrison. In the inland valley to the far north he established relations with Hamath. Having led the slaughter of thousands of fighters in the lands about, he thus completely surrounded and engulfed the highland heartland of "early" Israel. His political control extended beyond the Negeb, whose tribal forces he patronized, where he established a border cult to mark his military barrier against Egypt. In his power he held, with an exceptionally uniform, though tenuous, authority, the Asian colonies of what had been New Kingdom Egypt. The European dream of conquest was fulfilled.

Though David was everywhere dreaded and often hated, nevertheless his followers were many, especially in Judah, and many were the benefits he bestowed upon them. He did not depend on the highland for his support, and may have favored Israelite villagers with lighter taxes than elsewhere in his empire. The ability of a king in a small Palestinian capital to mobilize military support depended on coercion and favors, especially the dispensation of land grants and rations to palace dependents. David's military retainers and court functionaries and bureaucrats expected lands for service; these he provided out of estates in the conquered lowlands and Transjordan, rather than native highlands.

Support for David also depended on encouraging a regional sacral identity in diverse localities. This he sponsored through the Levites, evidently an Israelite tribe of priestly specialists notorious for their brutal allegiance to tribal ideals and authority. David assigned sections of the Levites domicile and pasture rights, but no land tenure, in forty-eight towns and villages, four for each tribe but not evenly distributed in the tribal territories. The Levitical towns were located mainly in frontier and lowland areas where David's rule was unfamiliar, and in Benjamin, where David seized the extensive lands of Saul's household. Most of all, support depended on the personal qualities of the king, and on his skill in publicizing the legitimacy of his kingship through architectural, ritual, and literary order, and through compounded personal success. For many in Judah, the early reign of David made possible a rising standard of living.

But by no means for all. David's opponents were numerous. Under his son's rule, the empire crumpled and upon his son's death collapsed altogether. David's unique kingdom was the object of his rivals' greed in his own day and of his heirs' vain memory in theirs. The scions of royal houses beaten and controlled by David rankled. Surviving members of the houses of Saul and Caleb sought revenge. Some of his own sons tried to overthrow him. The most notorious was Abishalom, supported in

Hebron by Amasa, a son of Yether and Abigail. Once Abishalom had been killed, David appointed Amasa to high position in his military, but then allowed him to be murdered. The villagers of Israel and Judah found David's rule no more agreeable than Saul's, against whom many had rebelled in David's favor. Popular resistance troubled David's reign and that of his son, and contributed decisively to his grandson's loss of everything but the kingdom of Judah. The revolt of the Bichrites behind Sheba anticipated the secession of Israel from the house of David a mere generation after the great king's death.

David was most successful in putting down the house of Saul. He kept Meribbaal and Mica in his care. When forced out of Jerusalem he took refuge in Saul's stronghold of Gilead, served by Barzillai ("Iron-man"), a strongman of Gilead and probably father of one of Saul's sons-in-law. Saul had once violated a tribal oath with the non-Israelite Gibeonites, and David had solicited their support. In return, they demanded the death of two of Saul's sons and five of his grandsons. The sons and grandsons were executed and their corpses exposed. Shimei, son of Gera of the house of Saul, publicly cursed David as a murderer damned by God. But David disregarded his curse for the moment, and when he arrived in Gilead was supplied by Barzillai, grandfather of five of the executed Saulids, who must have been dreadfully intimidated.[5]

By necessity David acceded to the entrenched tribal habits of his Judahite and Israelite subjects. In any case, the office of king brought him the support of a complicated network of clients. He had little need for further social control over the highland countryside. He issued no major body of law, but with the evident exception of blood feud allowed tribal custom to hold sway. Might was his right, and where royal order did not require his might, jurisdiction could run its tribal course. Joab's tribal militia played a role in his military strategy, but David's personal guard and private cohort supplied the more essential weapon. David taxed labor for strengthening his fortress in Jerusalem. That his subjects insisted on their tribal identity and customs made little difference beyond giving him the opportunity to grant the popular wish to maintain them.

David's administration operated on two tracks, tribal and state. The tribal sector was patterned after highland tradition, the state sector after Egyptian models. The military was under two heads. Joab headed the tribal militia, Benaiah the royal guard of Cerethites and Pelethites, that is, European Cretans and Aegean men, kin to if not identical with the Philistines. The cult was likewise under two heads. One was Abiathar, the sole survivor of the house of Eli, which presided over the Israelite cult of Shiloh and guarded the Israelite mobile battle palladium, the chest (ark) of Yahweh. He supervised David's pilgrimage cults, especially the border cult in the Sinai, where the threat from Egypt was the greatest, and possibly also the cults of the dispersed Levites. A priest named Zadok supervised the cult of the house of David in Jerusalem. Both cults were conducted in tent shrines, as far as is known, again in deference to the tribal sensibilities of highland and wasteland subjects.

The state god was Yahweh, a venerable manifestation of El, the divine warrior of tribal Israel. The name Yahweh, an apocopated, or shortened, sentence-name with El, was the way the tribes of Palestine under the umbrella of Israel referred to the tribal god El. That the tribes' god was El is clear from the name Israel, "El commands (the tribal forces)." In other words, Yahweh was the particular form that El took as the main god of the affiliated tribes. Of course El remained a member in good standing in the pantheons of the rest of Palestine as well. The tribal groups and members also referred to El as Elohim, an honorific plural of El.

The cults, both modest and distant, epitomized the state's ability to move quickly and strike decisively, often fatally, wherever required. Benaiah and Zadok, heading the state half of David's military and cult, were the sons of Jehoiada of Qabseel in the Negeb. They went back to David's earliest military successes as a wilderness brigand. They played a key role not only during David's rule, but during Solomon's as well, whose kingmakers they were. They represented the priestly family of Aaron, which apparently competed during the monarchic period with a priestly family of Moses, in an obscure rivalry generating only vague hints in the Scriptures. Some of David's seventeen sons also served as priests. The administration included also a head scribe, Shawsa, whose name was either Egyptian, like that of David's state priestly family, or Hurrian, as befitted the scribal tradition of Jerusalem going back to the Amarna period in the fourteenth century, and a royal herald named Joshaphat.

DAVID'S COURT WRITINGS

Literature from David's court formed the core of what became the Hebrew Scriptures. This court and cult literature was meant for the eyes and ears of the elite—always potential rivals—who were in his court or invited to it to lay down their potentially hostile arms. Only a tiny fraction of the people of Palestine knew what it said or cared.

Defense of Usurpation.   A history of David's overthrow of the house of Saul, now contained in approximately 1 Samuel 15—2 Samuel 5, was written to defend against charges that David was disloyal to Saul, or a deserter, a willful outlaw, a traitor, or that he had anything to do with Saul's, Abner's, or Ishbaal's deaths, or that any compulsion or god other than Yahweh was behind his success. This composition was meant to impress the Israelite sheikhs who were loyal to the house of Saul but were forced to support David after the murder of Ishbaal.

The sheikhs also knew about David's execution of the seven Saulids. How did David explain that? A second composition, much shorter, now found in 2 Sam. 21:1-14 and 2 Samuel 9, showed that David acted out of public necessity, under divine orders, to end a famine, that he arranged for the proper burial of the dead, and that he kept the Saulid Meribbaal in his care not under house arrest, but as proof of his goodwill.

A third composition, now 2 Samuel 13–20, demonstrated that Abishalom's rebellion could be traced to private not public causes, the reckless acts of individuals beyond David's control, and that David tried to prevent the killing of Abishalom and grieved profusely when the tragedy occurred. This was meant for Abishalom's Judahite backers under Amasa, who were encouraged into David's fold when Amasa was hired by his erstwhile enemy.

History of "Nation" and Cult: J.   Such defensive narratives disclose little about pre-Davidic Israel, but they do illustrate the political concern and audience that lay behind the main writings stemming from David's court. Shortly after setting up in Jerusalem, however, David ordered a history of early Israel written, starting with the creation of the world and human beings. This writing is known to historians as J, and the writer sometimes as the Yahwist. It comprises much of Genesis and Exodus and some of Numbers, and is the Bible's first history.

This writing had several purposes. It began by setting the history of Israel within a universal framework, provided by literary traditions regarding early humanity and the great flood. By David's time, these traditions had been known already for centuries in cuneiform texts still available in Palestine, although the pictorial alphabet had prevailed as the preferred method of writing in the courts of Palestine. Such a framework was appropriate for a court out to challenge the sovereignty of Egypt.

Another purpose was to appeal to the continued loyalty of the tribal sheikhs of the Negeb who had contributed to David's rise to power and frequented his court in Hebron, and who now played an essential role in the defense of his border with Egypt. David came to power in the south of Palestine, in the Negeb and the Philistine plain. He allied himself to forces in this area and the Sinai. When he was established, he made these allies the focus of the "national" history of Israel. David's history suggested to them that they themselves represented the ancestral heads of David's nation, which had, after all, a tribal background. But according to this history, the eponymous patriarchs of tribal Israel were Negeb nomadic sheikhs, the likes of Abram, Isaac, and Jacob, and not long-standing highland sheikhs or their presettlement antecedents, let alone their village bondsmen and working servants.

As often pointed out, Abram, Isaac, and perhaps Jacob were not part of the traditional genealogy of tribal Israel. Abram and Isaac, both of the south, were given priority over Jacob, for whom evidence suggests a possible earlier historical connection with tribal Israel. Abram was portrayed, moreover, as migrating from the far east solely because David's historian, as an urban cleric, employed cuneiform sources originating in Mesopotamia rather than Palestinian folk traditions for his history of early humanity, and thus at the appearance of Abram had to shift the scene from Mesopotamia to Palestine. Although the historian successfully integrated Abram's migration into his larger work, and was able to take advantage of the precedent of the original Israelite as an outsider being presented by God with all Palestine, nevertheless the extremely brief episode of migration was coincidental.

The twelve names of the tribes of Israel were traditional, but there is no reason to believe they formed a twelve-tribe group before David and his court conceived of them as such. Tribes that were previously tied only loosely if at all to Israel, such as Judah, were made integral. Indeed, Judah was made an eponymous hero in the history commissioned by David. Moreover, the tribes that were historically the least ancient territories in the Israelite affiliation, especially in the south, were made the oldest in David's history. These were the tribes born to Leah— Reuben, Simeon, Levi, Judah, Issachar, and Zebulun. Leah's slave Zilpah bore Gad and Asher, two crucial Davidic territories, also settled late by Israelites. Joseph and Benjamin, representing the original heartland of highland Israel, were born last, and Ephraim and Manasseh, not even of the same generation, were sons of an Egyptian mother, a problematic status in J's scheme of things. Clearly J is not recording early Israelite folklore.

So far as the narrative was not invented by David's scribe, its traditions about Abram and his descendants were tribal, but mostly not Israelite. David had no problem coping with the tribal nature of Judah and Israel: the antistate sentiment that imbued tribal lore lent itself readily to royal ideology. According to J, such an antitribal cult as that of a temple, for example, was excoriable; only modest sacrifices, requiring modest contributions, on field stone altars, were valid, even for the (Davidic) state.

The tribes tended to fight each other, the official history allowed, but by following the pattern of royal deference modeled especially by Abram they were able to compose their differences in order to present a united front against their worst foreign enemy, Egypt. The most difficult agreement was between the upstart south, Judah, and the highland heart of Israel, Joseph; their conflict was resolved through the deferential virtue of David's eponymous ancestor Judah. Under David, Israel had resolved its conflict with the European coalition and now depended on European forces. The new enemy was Egypt. The new official history therefore reversed the traditional Israelite attitudes toward the Philistines and Egypt: henceforth the Philistines were to be loved and the Egyptians hated. The primal event of nation formation was escape from jeopardy of *corvée* under Egypt in the delta, a harm far more likely to afflict the Negeb nomad than the highland villager. J amplified its anti-Egyptian theme in its thunderous conclusion because such antipathy became unalloyed policy in political Israel for the first time with David.

The complaints and revolts against the authoritative, kinglike rule of the revered Moses were numerous but illegitimate, J asserted: such singular saviors of Israel from the snares of the evil empire, whether Moses or, by implication, David, were to be respected and obeyed. The narrative of Moses, though possibly not the name, belonged to southern Palestine pastoral nomads; the name and narrative may have been merged for the first time by David's historian. The history concluded by showing that any attempt to reverse the sacral legitimation of such rule and the blessings it brought, endorsed by vassal kings, would outrage none other than the divine creator, the god of David's state and, in this composition's contention, nation.

The term nation fits David's subjects scarcely less poorly than it fits their tribal predecessors. As a social reality it belongs mainly to the industrial era. As noted in chapter 1, in ancient times the political consensus designated by "people" or "nation" was either projected by the ruler to reflect some social grouping of importance to him, as was the case with J, or it was a function of the hierarchy of clientship. Other criteria for a nation, such as people sharing an overarching political or cultural identity or simply recognizing each other as of the same political species apart from their allegiance to the monarch, do not pertain to David's kingdoms. The villagers of the highland spoke dialects of Palestinian Semitic, with local variations. The Hebrew used in David's court was a southern variety that only a small minority of Israelites would have recognized as their own. David's Israelite subjects engaged in cultural exchange to some extent, but there were few if any sharp boundaries in the cultural continuum with their non-Israelite neighbors, and exchange over any distance at all was of doubtful value to most villagers. As for mutual recognition, this notion also is better treated in terms of clientship and jurisdiction, and the term Israel understood in political or legal terms, just as was the case with tribal Israel.

Ancient Songs and Blessings.   Besides presenting the Bible's first history, J incorporates a women's victory song (Exodus 15), an itemized blessing of the individual tribes (Genesis 49), and four blessings of Israel as a single entity (Numbers 23–24), all of which appear to reflect, if not exactly reproduce, pre-Davidic compositions of the eleventh century. Miriam's song posits the tribal opposition of highland and lowland. Yahweh covers Egypt's chariot forces with the sea and leaves the chiefs of all Israel's lowland and highland opponents in utter dismay: Philistines, Edomites, Moabites, and opposing Palestinians. The song concludes as Yahweh leads his people to their highland sanctuary, which is referred to as though there were only one. If J retouched the song, the sanctuary appears to be the shrine of David's cult in Jerusalem.

Jacob's blessing of the tribes in Genesis 49 is in archaic form, though significant parts of it, including the order of the tribes and several of the points made about them, make sense only in terms of the specific propaganda of J itself. Judah and Joseph receive the main attention. Judah is assigned a royal destiny, while Joseph is acknowledged as the most productive of the tribes. The tribal areas are sometimes closely defined: Zebulun reaches the coast and extends as far as Sidon, Issachar falls under *corvée* duty, an indication they are vulnerable at least in part to the predations of lowland lords, and Dan lies across the tradeways, in the north. Whether these reflect the eleventh or tenth century may be uncertain. Balaam's blessings portray a numerous highland tribal affiliation, dwelling in tents consistent with their trek in the main narrative. Direct reference is made to Agag of the Amalekites and an Israelite king, so they cannot date from much before the tenth century. The reference in Balaam's blessings to Israel coming out of Egypt probably also results from their placement in J.

Prayers of the Afflicted. The liturgy of David's private cult, the official cult of the state, consisted of sung prayers to Yahweh modeled on the traditional folk prayer to the divine patron of the unjustly accused and persecuted individual, a type of speech itself patterned after the patron-client relations on which villagers depended. Day after day, month after month, year after year, David, or a priestly client or son as his liturgical surrogate, voiced the cares of his little empire by recalling the pleas he made in his outlaw days, when his pursuers were many and he spoke for and attracted to his band villagers freighted with unjust debt and unable to obtain redress from their Israelite masters and their cohort. In dire straits, David used to intone the typical cry of the oppressed plaintiff to Yahweh. Yahweh had obviously answered his cry and delivered him. Prayers of this kind had worked for David; hence he made them the basis of his regular attendance in the court of his god for the rest of his life. If any of his lowly subjects happened to discover what their king sang to his god, they could rest assured the king knew their condition and would faithfully present their own plea, oft repeated in local cults throughout the land, in the highest court of all. These royal complaints were recorded and became the core of the biblical psalter.

Other Works.   In addition there are several fragments of court documents in the Bible, including lists of court officers, isolated war annals, lists of fighters, and a brief history of the palladium that explains how it fell into Philistine hands but was then returned to Israel and finally introduced into Jerusalem. The pro-David narratives in Judges 17–21 may come from David's court. The fighter lists reveal the nature of David's Palestinian troops no later than his rule in Hebron; they do not show his dependence on his European guard. David's Palestinian fighters were ranked by exploit and seniority. They were headed by "the three": Yeshbaal killed eight hundred Philistines at one time, Eleazar held his ground when his fellows retreated and killed Philistines "until his hand stuck to his sword," and Shamma held a lentil plot when all others fled and beat the Philistines by himself. Two men did not attain to "the three," but were nevertheless revered above others: Abishai was made commander of David's private troop, and Benaiah, known for killing a lion in a pit and an Egyptian with the man's own spear, was put in charge of his bodyguard. In the troop itself, fighters from Bethlehem and vicinity, tracing their loyalty to David's term with Saul and earliest outlaw days, tended to rank highest. They were followed by a group of fighters from north of Bethlehem, also attracted to David during his fight with Saul against the Philistines. The early elite fighters were filled out with a mercenary squad of pastoral tribalists from east of Gilead, an Ammonite, two Ithrites from Qiryat-yearim between Jerusalem and Gezer, and Uriah the Hittite. In sum, the core of David's native band consisted mostly of men from near his home, from the area of his early exploits in Benjamin and Judah, and mercenaries from the Shephelah and Gath. Only one came from the area north of Benjamin under the nominal control of the house of Saul.

Thus the picture of early Israel composed for David and his court results from the ambiguous outcome of the long struggle between highland and lowland: a highland warlord won the war, but his economic base became largely lowland. David embodied the victory of outlying Palestinians and of European forces over Israel. Through the defeat of both Saul and the Philistines, David completed the European conquest of Israel. His son Solomon, guided by Zadok and Benaiah from the extreme south, would consummate David's conquest in the Israelite temple state.

LATER SCRIPTURES

The subsequent history of the Hebrew Scriptures and their references to early Israel can be sketched in general outline. At the death of Solomon, the chiefs of the traditional territories of highland Israel overthrew the house of David. The house of David was reduced to the rule of Judah, a fragment of the erstwhile empire of David. The Israelite usurper, Jeroboam, adopted the official history of Israel, J, from the royal archives and had it recopied with revisions that reflected his own career and concerns. These revisions, known as E, neither incorporate folk tradition nor relate anything about early Israel. Indeed, for the most part they ignore the tribal character of J's Israel.

Deuteronomistic History.   Two centuries later the kingdom of Israel fell to Assyria and was never restored. The house of David in Judah came to terms with Assyria and survived as an Assyrian vassal. When in the late seventh century, under King Josiah, it finally threw off the Assyrian yoke, it looked to reconquer Israel and to reincorporate it into a restored and enlarged Davidic temple state. Since the official Davidic history of Israel, however, had made no mention of the temple, indeed had scorned the very idea of a temple, it was necessary for Josiah's scribes to compose a new history of Israel, which showed that the temple in Jerusalem was indeed essential to God's plan from the beginning, that being ruled by a Davidic king was better than any alternative, and that the law promulgated by Josiah in Jerusalem was the law of the tribal hero Moses. This history incorporated several extant defenses of usurpation, especially David's and Jehu's, a local saints' history of the Israelite monarchy, and excerpts from royal archives, and is now found in the books of Deuteronomy through 2 Kings, excluding Ruth.

This so-called Deuteronomistic history partitions events from the exodus to Josiah into discrete periods. The first three periods purport to depict premonarchic Israel and have had a profound influence on later concepts of early Israel. The first period consists of Moses' last day alive. He delivers Yahweh's law, arranges to have it written down, prescribes its periodic recitation, and dies. In the second period, Joshua studies this written law assiduously and leads his people in unity to great victory and the conquest of most of the territory of Israel as conceived of by Josiah. Joshua is modeled on Josiah, and his conquest on Josiah's murderous rampage through the highland in the attempt to recover the glory of David's kingdom. In the third period, the law seems to have been misplaced. No one refers to it. There is no king, and, contrary to the prescription of the law, no central shrine where all Israel can repair to meet Yahweh. The result is political chaos—an object lesson to those who might be tempted to dispense with the house of David. The disorder of this period is resolved only with the appointment of not just any king, but the king who was to conquer Jerusalem and whose son was to build the temple that secured the Israelite political order that was the divine intention all along. The period of the Judges as conventionally conceived is simply the third period of this Josianic scheme.

Deborah's Song. The traditions that are incorporated to enhance points made in the Books of Joshua and Judges are earlier than Josiah—sometimes much earlier. Whether they predate David is another question. In the case of one text, the answer is almost certainly yes. The victory song of Deborah (Judges 5) may be the oldest composition in the Hebrew Scriptures. It alludes to an affiliation of nine or ten tribes, of which the five or six closest to the Jezreel valley join in a battle to defeat a lowland chariot force, led by a European commander named Sisera, dispatched to put a stop to tribal raiding of caravans. The tribes win, and the last scene depicts Sisera's wife and mother imagining his neck bedecked with variegated cloths, whereas in fact it is dripping with his own gore. The battle is consummated by a woman, who single-handedly kills Sisera in her own tent. In this song Israel consists of *perazon* (RSV, "peasantry"), apparently denoting a village population. The tribes lying farther away refuse the call to battle, and the song taunts them for their cowardice. As Stager suggests, they stay out from economic self-interest: their interest lies with maritime trade (Dan and Asher) and specialized pastoralism (Reuben and Gilead), both activities that are less autarkic than highland subsistence. Judah is not mentioned at all. The song is propaganda for a common tribal enterprise, first recorded in some chief's court, and thus illustrates the expected lack of common identity and purpose among the tribes even among the elite.

Strongmen. The prose traditions of Joshua and Judges concern local warlords, ruffians, and saints who were originally heroes of antiroyal sentiment but have been co-opted into Josiah's history, probably from an earlier document. Without their literary frames, they reflect the attitude that people can fend for themselves without a king. For Josiah, the stories in Judges show the political uncertainty and insecurity that result from the lack of a strong king of Israel ruling from Jerusalem. Josiah's historian used an earlier document that contained only northern, or Israelite, traditions, from Ehud to Samson of Dan and Samuel of Benjamin. Again Judah is missing, the story of Othniel (Judg. 3:7-11) being a separate, possibly Deuteronomistic composition. The prior collection preserves tribal values. The stories are not anti-Davidic, probably because the house of David selected and preserved them. They describe local, ad hoc military responses against superior forces, and heroic feats of lone warriors and outlaw saviors. Not one portrays an Israel-wide movement. This is both in character for such lore, and in the Deuteronomist's interest in saving the all-Israelite solution for the Davidic monarchy.

The problems faced by these heroes are indicative of the perennially decentralized conditions in the highland, whether under the governance of a tribal chief or weak king. Most (not all) could have originated at many possible times in the four centuries between Saul and Josiah, rather than in early Israel. Ehud rescues Benjaminites from having to pay tribute to a Transjordanian tribal warlord. Shamgar kills six hundred Philistines with an oxgoad. In a prose version of the battle described in Deborah's victory song, Deborah of Ephraim fights in Jezreel. The Palestinian warlord behind Sisera is said to have his residence in Hazor. Such a picture could only fit Hazor XI, which dates to the end of the eleventh century at the earliest, suggesting that this element of the prose account was nearly contemporary with David or later. Gideon of Manasseh resists tribal raids from the Transjordan—Midianites, Ishmaelites, eastern tribes (6:3)—in probably the best example of a narrative describing the local defense of production. In the story of Abimelek and his seventy brothers, Jotham presents a suitably tribal, antiroyal parable; but the story is tied to Shechem at a time when it is known to have been unoccupied. Again, the narrative apparently stems from around the time of David and was preserved as propaganda in the king's or chieftain's court. Tola is an Issacharite living in Ephraim. Is this where the tribe of Issachar lived until the traditional territory of Issachar was settled at the beginning of the monarchic period? Jair of Gilead is a wealthy chief of Gilead. Jephthah of Gilead is a local ruffian savior against the Ammonites. Ibzan is a resident of Bethlehem, which was probably a late settlement. Elon of Zebulun and Abdon the Priathonite of Ephraim are little more than names. The struggles of Samson of Dan are the most developed of the group. Not surprisingly, they epitomize, in folkloric fashion, the conflict between highlander and lowlander, the rough-and-ready who, as Bynum explains, bumps, jostles, jars, pushes, and shoves against the refined and civilized.

These narratives of local heroes illustrate the conditions of tribal life in the highlands without for the most part using tribal idiom or rooting historically in the early Israelite period. With few exceptions, what they might reveal to us about conditions in early Israel could be surmised from the historical information in the compositions of the reign of David, archaeological data, ethnographic parallels, and the comparative historical geography of Palestine. The barest narrative history of early Israel awaits the many archaeological discoveries yet to be made.

CHAPTER EIGHT

The End
of Early Israel

Israel originated as the name for a complex, variable tribal affiliation of Palestinian farmers and pastoralists under the lordship of tribal sheikhs, in the north of Palestine and around Hazor and possibly Bethshan. As an organized power, Israel grew in official importance during the thirteenth century B.C.E., when Egypt dealt with Israel's tribal heads to create a semi-cooperative surrogate force in the border zone between the Egyptian and Hittite imperial spheres. The fall of Hatti, the incursion of Europeans, and the fall of Egypt in Palestine sparked and then fueled the spread of tribal villages under tribal aegis on the highland frontiers of settlement during the twelfth century, much but not all of which was overseen by the empowered chiefs of Israel. As European lords came to dominate the Palestinian lowland, especially in the second half of the twelfth century, the Israelite center of gravity shifted to the highland of central Palestine, in what was later defined as the territories of Manasseh, Ephraim, and Benjamin.

By the end of the twelfth century, the two main groups of erstwhile Egyptian surrogates held their territories. The

Europeans were in control of the coast, of Bethshan and its territory, and of parts of the Jordan valley, and the chiefs of Israel were in control of the central highlands. Both camps included elements of the Palestinian elite of the New Kingdom period. In the late twelfth and eleventh centuries, the emerging regional pattern of conflict pitted the lords of the lowland against those of the highland, whose forces were an irritation and whose lands an invitation, in a struggle for sovereignty over the whole of Palestine. The lords of the lowland confederated in an attempt to match and overcome the highland tribes of Israel.

By the end of the eleventh century, the Europeans looked set to win the struggle. They had, however, helped to establish a highland outlaw named David, who, from his base in the frontier of the Negeb and Judah and with the help of European mercenaries, surrounded Israel and captured it himself, thus turning the tables on the lowland lords and claiming sovereignty over greater Palestine, with many lowland Europeans still in place, in the name of the tribes of Israel. David's court history of Israel, the basis of the later biblical narrative, mirrored his relations with forces in the territories where he rose to power and his opposition to Egypt, and ignored as irrelevant most of what might have been remembered, however vaguely, about the historical origin of Israel by the settlers or their northern chiefs.

Israel thus originated wholly within the framework of typical political relations in Palestine. There was no golden age of Israel. Early Israel embodied no ideal traits. The politics of tribal Israel included many of the elements characteristic of Palestinian city-state society, especially in the thirteenth and late eleventh centuries. Nevertheless the new tribal settlements seemed more inviting to many farming families and groups than life under Egyptian or

Philistine rule, not least because they provided the option of indigenous rule, or nominal self-rule, in contrast to foreign rule, whether by Egyptians or Europeans. The expansion of settlement provided relatively improved conditions in some respects for the poor farming families of Israel and their chiefs, in the period sandwiched between the New Kingdom and the house of David, who along with his successor Solomon practically destroyed tribal organization in Israel. The characteristics of highland tribal Israel in the twelfth and eleventh centuries—whether political, economic, social, or religious—were the reflex of a Palestinian tribal organization in a highland settlement frontier under pressure from a lowland military. Many examples of such a development could be pointed out, and none of them would provide occasion for idealizing the lives and choices of the settlers.

There was nothing mysterious about the origin of Israel and nothing miraculous about it, other than the mystery of vitality and enterprise in the face of oppression and the miracle of resistance to tyranny. These are mysteries and miracles that occur all the time, though they are no less mysterious or miraculous for that. Thus they do not bestow on the origin of Israel a unique or even distinctive character. Nor does the tragedy of early Israel, that its vitality and resistance should be achieved in so many mutually contradictory ways.

The origin of Israel therefore puts an end to early Israel as a concept imbued with ethnic tenaciousness, legal justice, ethical purity, fighting courage, or religious faith. With respect to the biblical period, the category "early Israel" derives from the simple contrast between Israel before the monarchy and Israel during and after the monarchy. In itself the category has little meaning other than "premonarchic Israel." To understand early Israel primarily in geopolitical terms, as this book does, is to elaborate on precisely this contrast. It is, furthermore, the most pertinent contrast, for it leads us directly into the complexities of the politics of tribes, where the concept of Israel first received its structure and substance.

What then of the faith of Israel? Did not the heightened religious consciousness of early Israel in time make possible the Hebrew Scriptures and the Christian Bible and the Jewish Talmud? Did not God's creation of early Israel, and early Israel's revelation of God, mark a new and therefore unique moment in human history? To locate the distinctiveness of the Scriptures and their theological revelation in the moment of Israel's origin takes both out of the realm of history. As such they become meaningless and susceptible to the manipulation of the self-justified. The distinctiveness of the Scriptures and of the communities of faith that produced them lies not in the origin of Israel or any other single moment in scriptural history, but in the course of the scriptural period, from earliest Israel to the present. Their meaning cannot be divorced from the historical process, all parts of which contributed to their role in our lives today, and to our knowledge of God.

The genius of the Bible springs not from its roots in tribal ethos, but from the inveterate critique and theodicy of the temple state perpetuated for century after century by the prophets of Israel and Judah, preserved in writing in the temple itself, and recalled and reincarnated by over one hundred generations since then. This critical perspective, even in its sacerdotal form, is based on the same miracle of resistance to oppression incarnated in tribal ethos. However, it is ongoing and its spirit vital in all times and places. It does not depend on perfect examples for its expression. There were many historical and ideological reasons for the court and temple clerics who produced the Hebrew Scriptures, and the synagogue and

church clerics who later interpreted them, to build continuously on David's quasitribal invalidation of the temple
state in J, keeping the critique of the temple state at the
heart of the Scriptures. Not the least was the fall of Jerusalem in the early sixth century B.C.E. and of the house
of David three generations later.

Whatever the reasons, the states of Israel and Judah and
the Persian province of Judah found it expedient to com-
promise with the critical resistance to oppression whose
self-evident truth had no equal. Moreover, this feature of
the Scriptures meant that, although when the temple fell
in 70 C.E. the temple Scriptures as such became a dead
letter, at the same time the scriptural faith that God's
justification exceeds the confines of the temple state lived
on, in its Jewish and Christian forms, which included the
new Scriptures of the Mishnah and New Testament. Thus
the rejection of the absolute supremacy of the state, which
was implied but imperfectly realized in Palestinian tribal
formations, survives as an essential component of the
faiths descended from the Hebrew Scriptures today.[1]

Notes

PREFACE

1. Robert B. Coote and Keith W. Whitelam, *The Emergence of Early Israel in Historical Perspective*. Sheffield: Almond Press, 1987.

2. Robert B. Coote and David Robert Ord, *The Bible's First History*. Philadelphia: Fortress Press, 1989.

INTRODUCTION

1. Albrecht Alt, "The Settlement of the Israelites in Palestine," in *Essays on Old Testament History and Religion* (Garden City, N.Y.: Doubleday, 1968), 173–221. See the excellent critique in Niels Peter Lemche, *Early Israel: Anthropological and Historical Studies on the Israelite Society Before the Monarchy* (Leiden: E. J. Brill, 1985), 35–48.

2. I take this to be the main theme of Norman Gottwald's *The Tribes of Yahweh: A Sociology of the Religion of Liberated Israel, 1250–1050* B.C.E. (Maryknoll, N.Y.: Orbis Books, 1979), despite the fact that it is open to the criticism of being itself idealistic. Numerous detractors have lodged this criticism, but the perception has not escaped sympathetic reviewers as well; see for example the review by Marvin L. Chaney in *Journal of Biblical Literature* 103 (1984): 93. Gottwald's more recent reflections can be seen in "Two Models for the Origins of Ancient Israel: Social Revolution or Frontier Development," in *The Quest for the Kingdom of God: Studies in Honor of George E. Mendenhall*, ed. H. B. Huffmon, F. A. Spina, and A. R. W. Green (Winona Lake, Ind.: Eisenbrauns, 1983), 5–24; "Religious Conversion and the Societal Origins of Ancient Israel,"

Perspectives in Religious Studies 15(1988): 49–65; "Israel's Emergence in Canaan: *BR* Interviews Norman Gottwald," *Bible Review* 5, no. 5 (October 1989): 26–34; "The Exodus as Event and Process: A Test Case in the Biblical Grounding of Liberation Theology," in *The Future of Liberation Theology: Essays in Honor of Gustavo Gutierrez,* ed. Marc H. Ellis and Otto Maduro (Maryknoll, N.Y.: Orbis Books, 1989), 250–60; and his forthcoming article on "Sociology of Ancient Israel" in the *Anchor Bible Dictionary.*

3. Albrecht Alt, "The Settlement of the Israelites in Palestine;" Martin Noth, *The History of Israel,* 2d ed. (N.Y.: Harper & Row, 1960), 1–163; George E. Mendenhall, "The Hebrew Conquest of Palestine," in *The Biblical Archaeologist* 25, no. 3 (September 1962), 66–87; Norman K. Gottwald, *The Tribes of Yahweh.* It would be misleading to imply that no one holds to such views, or to the assumptions behind them, any longer. This is far from the case. The socio-political contexts in which these views were formulated continue to exert a strong influence on the study of early Israel. As an example, Bryant Wood's "Did the Israelites Conquer Jericho? A New Look at the Archaeological Evidence," *Biblical Archaeology Review* 16, no. 2 (March/April 1990): 44–58 is noteworthy not just for its significant scholarly contribution to a possible revision of the prevailing view of the occupation of Late Bronze Age Jericho, but for its resonant echo in the public media in the United States. The American public was eager to follow Wood's leading question, "If the Hyksos did not destroy Jericho and the Egyptians did not destroy Jericho, then who did?" (p. 53). "Evidence Supports the Bible," cheered headlines across the country, illustrating the tenacity of the neoconservative assumptions of American and Israeli biblical archaeology that sustained the conquest model of Israel's origins in the 1940s, 1950s, and 1960s. Other scholars continue to accept the infiltration and revolution models in their essentials as well.

4. The chronology of the Egyptian New Kingdom continues to be the subject of debate. In this book I adopt the lowest, or latest, of the proposed chronologies, which seems to enjoy the current support of the majority of historians.

5. *Early Israel,* 414.

6. *Oxford Bible Atlas,* 3d ed. (New York: Oxford University Press, 1984), *The Harper Atlas of the Bible* (New York: Harper & Row, 1987).

CHAPTER 1

1. The purpose of such a portrait is to make explicit my assumptions about Palestinian society as a whole in the period covered by this book. Moreover, as early "Israelites" were not culturally different from other inhabitants of Palestine, this portrait places the early Israelites from the start in a definite cultural context. As mentioned in the introduction, this chapter clarifies in particular the political structure of Palestinian society in the Late Bronze and Early Iron Ages, an essential component of a view that takes seriously the basically political nature of early Israel. The most controversial issue addressed here is the importance of class struggle in the history of early Israel. Most

scholars would probably still prefer to disregard class struggle as a factor altogether. My own view is that as the underlying theme of agrarian history it is an essential factor, but it does not as such explain the historical changes that led to the emergence of Israel as a tribal power and monarchy.

2. Miriam Lichtheim, *Ancient Egyptian Literature*. Vol. 2; *The New Kingdom* (Berkeley: University of California Press, 1976), 170–71.

3. The inevitable conflict between state and landed nobility is probably a significant variation on elite rivalry rather than a separate political dynamic. See the recent conception of Chris Wickham, "The Uniqueness of the East," in *Europe and the Rise of Capitalism*, ed. Jean Baechler, John A. Hall, and Michael Mann (Cambridge, Mass.: Basil Blackwell, 1988), 66–100.

CHAPTER 2

1. James B. Pritchard, ed., *Ancient Near Eastern Texts Relating to the Old Testament*, 2d ed. (Princeton: Princeton University Press, 1955), 237 (henceforth abbreviated *ANET*).

2. Ibid., 238.

3. Ibid., 239.

4. Ibid., 239.

5. Canaan referred to the inhabited areas of Palestine and southern coastal Lebanon. The Egyptians used Canaan as one of several terms to designate a portion of their Asian empire. In this sense, Israelites were Canaanites. In this book I use Palestine to refer to a territory, people, and culture, where most scholars continue to use Canaan, even though the two terms are not exactly equivalent. The reason is important: since in the Bible and in plain English "Canaan" connotes a contrast to "Israel," an alien entity against which "Israel" struggles for survival, the continued use of Canaan for prebiblical Palestine is extremely problematic and misleading, implying in the worst instance that prebiblical Israel was indeed located somewhere other than in Palestine. Some would argue, however, that the remedy is worse than the disease: what sense, after all, does it make to suggest that Israelites were "Palestinians"? Leaving aside modern national categories, the usage in this book has the advantage of making the reader stop and think rather than assuming without reflection the biblical nomenclature and its underlying ideology. See the remarks of Joe D. Seger in *Biblical Archaeology Today: Proceedings of the International Congress on Biblical Archaeology, Jerusalem, April 1984* (Jerusalem: Israel Exploration Society, 1985), 157–58, and Michael D. Coogan, in *Ancient Israelite Religion: Essays in Honor of Frank Moore Cross*, ed. Patrick D. Miller, Jr., Paul D. Hanson, and S. Dean McBride (Philadelphia: Fortress Press, 1987), 121 n. 5.

6. *ANET*, 485; William L. Moran, *Les lettres d'El Amarna: Correspondance diplomatique du pharaon* (Paris: Les Editions du Cerf, 1987), 560–61.

7. *ANET*, 247 (adapted).

8. Moshe Dothan, "Terminology for the Archaeology of the Biblical Periods," in *Biblical Archaeology Today: Proceedings of the International Congress on*

Biblical Archaeology, Jerusalem, April 1984 (Jerusalem: Israel Exploration Society, 1985), 139.

9. These may have predated Ramesses III, especially at Gaza, the Egyptian capital of Palestine.

CHAPTER 3

1. The study of regional patterns of settlement in the Middle East is in its infancy, but is already proving to be of great significance in understanding factors and circumstances for which there is little or no written evidence. As settlement studies grow in importance, biblical historians continue to broaden their understanding of the history of the biblical period to include the many facets of historical geography.

2. Rivka Gonen, "Urban Canaan in the Late Bronze Period," *Bulletin of the American Schools of Oriental Research* 253 (1984): 68.

CHAPTER 4

1. The term rendered "Canaan" in many earlier translations is now thought to refer to the chief town of Canaan, Gaza. This change appears to invalidate the interesting structural study of this text by Gösta W. Ahlström and Diana Edelman, "Merneptah's Israel," *Journal of Near Eastern Studies* 44 (1985): 59–61, in which Canaan and Israel are opposed; similarly Gösta W. Ahlström, *Who Were the Israelites?* (Winona Lake, Ind.: Eisenbrauns, 1986), 37–45. The translation "Canaan" is retained by Frank Yurco, "3,200-Year-Old Picture of Israelites Found in Egypt." *Biblical Archaeology Review* 16, no. 5 (September/October 1990): 20–38. Yurco's significant contribution is center of important debate.

2. Michael E. Meeker, *Literature and Violence in North Arabia* (Cambridge: Cambridge University Press, 1979), 191.

3. Ibid., 192.

4. Ibid., 192.

5. Finkelstein seems to favor an ethnic concept of early Israel, even though he refers to the individual tribes as such. Such a concept of early Israel may rest on an assumption of ethnic uniformity, which without further close examination may be inappropriate to the study of ancient agrarian, or prenationalist, societies, but admittedly difficult to dispel or replace in modern academic contexts. This question, however, requires much further research. Yurco's insistence that "Israelites" could not be *shasu* is unnecessary as "Israelites" could have been both non-*shasu* and *shasu*.

6. *ANET*, 254.

7. Ibid., 254.

8. Ibid., 248.

9. A similar suggestion is made by Ernst Axel Knauf, *Midian: Untersuchungen zur Geschichte Palästinas und Nordarabiens am Ende des 2. Jahrtausends v. Chr.* (Wiesbaden: Otto Harrassowitz, 1988), 97–99, 135–38.

10. Walter P. Zenner, "Aqiili Agha: The Strongman in the Ethnic Relations of the Ottoman Galilee," *Comparative Studies in Society and History* 14 (1972): 183.

CHAPTER 5

1. The names of particular "sea peoples" appear to have designated groups possessing a common place of origin as much as anything. Some may have shared dialect and customs as well, which in an alien context such as the eastern Mediterranean coastal regions might have produced an identity akin to the modern sense of ethnic identity. It is important to note, however, that, apart from pictorial representations, the different "sea peoples" are not so far distinguishable from one another in the archaeological record.

2. Richmond Lattimore, *The Odyssey of Homer* (New York: Harper & Row, 1965), 217.

3. *ANET*, 262–63.

4. Ibid., paraphrased.

5. Ibid., 262.

6. The transition from MycIIIC1b one-color ware to Philistine two-color ware was gradual, unlike the cessation of imported ware, an indication that the same alien group was the main producer of both local wares.

7. It even appears as far away as Sardinia and Sicily, as the "sea peoples" migrated west as well as east.

8. In some localities it was more common. In the kiln area at T. Miqneh, the local MycIIIC1b ware made up two-thirds of the pottery. See Trude Dothan, "Ekron of the Philistines: Part I: Where They Came From, How They Settled Down and the Place They Worshiped In," *Biblical Archaeology Review* 16, no. 1 (January/February 1990): 27.

CHAPTER 6

1. Israel Finkelstein, *The Archaeology of the Israelite Settlement* (Jerusalem: Israel Exploration Society, 1988), 15 n. 1 and passim.

2. Douglas L. Esse, review of Finkelstein, *The Archaeology of the Israelite Settlement, Biblical Archaeology Review* 14, no. 5 (September/October 1988): 12.

3. Bryant Wood's evidence for reanalyzing the settlement history of Jericho does not, of course, significantly affect this conclusion; see above, Introduction n. 3.

4. See Adam Zertal, "Has Joshua's Altar Been Found on Mt. Ebal?" *Biblical Archaeology Review* 11, no. 1 (January/February 1985): 26–43; A. Kempinski, "Joshua's Altar—An Iron Age I Watchtower," *Biblical Archaeology Review* 12, no. 1 (January/February 1986): 42, 44–49; Zertal, "How Can Kempinski Be So Wrong?" *Biblical Archaeology Review* 12, no. 1 (January/February 1986): 43, 49–53; William G. Dever, "The Contribution of Archaeology to the Study of Canaanite and Early Israelite Religion," in *Ancient Israelite Religion: Essays in Honor of Frank Moore Cross*, ed. Patrick D. Miller, Jr., Paul D. Hanson, and S.

Dean McBride (Philadelphia: Fortress Press, 1987), 233, 245 n. 66. Similar problems of interpretation surround the possible shrine reported in Amihai Mazar, "The 'Bull Site'—An Iron Age I Open Cult Place," *Bulletin of the American Schools of Oriental Research* 247 (1982): 27–42. The "Israelite" character of this site is questioned by Michael D. Coogan, *Palestine Exploration Quarterly* 119 (1987): 1–8; for Mazar's response, see "On Cult Places and Early Israelites: A Response to Michael Coogan," *Biblical Archaeology Review* 15, no. 4 (July/ August 1988): 45. See also R. Wenning and E. Zenger, "Ein bäuerliches Baal-Heiligtum im samarischen Gebirge aus der Zeit der Anfänge Israels," *Zeitschrift des Deutschen Palästina-Vereins* 102 (1986): 75–86.

CHAPTER 7

1. It may be fair to say that as questions about early Israel reach some resolution, pending major new sources of archaeological data, the albeit related issue of the origin of what the Scriptures say about early Israel will continue to spark as much debate and disagreement as ever. What follows is a summary of my current understanding of this issue, much of which is laid out in more detail in the works under my name in the Bibliography (pp. 178, 182–85).

2. The discussion of the role of the domestication of the camel in the formation of Israel has reached a new level of sophistication in H. Keith Beebe, "The Dromedary Revolution," Occasional Papers of The Institute for Antiquity and Christianity, 18 (Claremont, Calif.: The Institute for Antiquity and Christianity, 1990), which appeared too late for use in this work.

3. Daniel Bates and Amal Rassam, *Peoples and Cultures of the Middle East* (Englewood Cliffs, N.J.: Prentice-Hall, 1983), 264.

4. Some take the title "Baal" in such names to refer to the "Lord" Yahweh.

5. These two Barzillais are usually treated as different persons, but were probably the same.

CHAPTER 8

1. For a concise overview of the formation of the Christian and Jewish Scriptures in their entirety, see Robert B. Coote and Mary P. Coote, *Power, Politics, and the Making of the Bible: An Introduction* (Minneapolis: Fortress Press, 1990).

Bibliography

In addition to the works cited here, the bibliographies of the more recent works, especially Finkelstein's, can direct the reader to further study. A few entries are listed under more than one chapter.

GENERAL

The following journals carry articles on the latest research related to early Israel:

Biblical Archaeologist, quarterly, Baltimore, Maryland.

Biblical Archaeology Review, bimonthly, Washington, D.C.

Bulletin of the American Schools of Oriental Research, quarterly, Baltimore, Maryland.

Israel Exploration Journal, quarterly, Jerusalem.

Zeitschrift des Deutschen Palästina Vereins, quarterly, Stuttgart.

CHAPTER 1

Baly, Denis, *Basic Biblical Geography*. Philadelphia: Fortress Press, 1987.

Bates, Daniel G., and Rassam, Amal. *Peoples and Cultures of the Middle East*. Englewood Cliffs, N.J.: Prentice-Hall, 1983.

Borowski, Oded. *Agriculture in Iron Age Israel*. Winona Lake, Ind.: Eisenbrauns, 1987.

Dalman, Gustav. *Arbeit und Sitte in Palästina*. 7 vols. 1928–1942. Reprint. Hildesheim: 1964–1971.

Bibliography

Eickelman, Dale F. *The Middle East: An Anthropological Approach*. Englewood Cliffs, N.J.: Prentice-Hall, 1981.

Gottwald, Norman K. "The Israelite Settlement as a Social Revolutionary Movement." In *Biblical Archaeology Today: Proceedings of the International Congress on Biblical Archaeology, Jerusalem, April 1984*. Jerusalem: Israel Exploration Society, 1985.

Grant, Elihu. *The Peasantry of Palestine: The Life, Manners and Customs of the Village*. Boston: The Pilgrim Press, 1907.

Kautsky, John H. *The Politics of Aristocratic Empires*. Chapel Hill: University of North Carolina Press, 1982.

Lemche, Niels Peter. *Early Israel: Anthropological and Historical Studies on the Israelite Society Before the Monarchy*. Leiden: E. J. Brill, 1985.

Lenski, Gerhard E. *Power and Privilege: A Theory of Social Stratification*. Chapel Hill: University of North Carolina Press, 1984.

Matthews, Victor H. *Manners and Customs in the Bible*. Peabody, Mass.: Hendrickson Publishers, 1988.

Paul, Shalom M., and Dever, William G., eds. *Biblical Archaeology*. New York: Quadrangle/The New York Times, 1974.

Pritchard, James B., ed. *Ancient Near Eastern Texts Relating to the Old Testament*, 3d ed. Princeton: Princeton University Press, 1969.

CHAPTER 2

Aharoni, Yohanan. *The Land of the Bible: A Historical Geography*, rev. ed. Philadelphia: Westminster Press, 1979.

Bienkowski, Piotr. "Prosperity and Decline in LBA Canaan: A Reply to Liebowitz and Knapp." *Bulletin of the American Schools of Oriental Research* 275 (1989): 59–63.

Bryce, Trevor R. "The Boundaries of Hatti and Hittite Border Policy." *Tel Aviv* 13–14 (1986–87): 85–102.

The Cambridge Ancient History, 3d ed. Vol. 2, Part 2, *History of the Middle East and the Aegean Region c. 1380—1000* B.C. Edited by I. E. S. Edwards, et al. Cambridge: Cambridge University Press, 1975.

Chaney, Marvin L. "Ancient Palestinian Peasant Movements and the Formation of Premonarchic Israel." In *Palestine in Transition: The Emergence of Ancient Israel*, ed. David Noel Freedman and David Frank Graf. Sheffield: Almond Press, 1983.

Görg, Manfred. *Beiträge zur Zeitgeschichte der Anfänge Israels: Dokumente, Materialien, Notizen*. Wiesbaden: Harrassowitz, 1989.

Gottwald, Norman K. *The Tribes of Yahweh: A Sociology of the Religion of Liberated Israel, 1250–1050* B.C.E. Maryknoll, N.Y.: Orbis Books, 1979.

Halpern, Baruch. *The Emergence of Israel in Canaan*. Chico, Calif.: Scholars Press, 1983.

James, T. G. H. *Pharaoh's People: Scenes from Life in Imperial Egypt.* Chicago: University of Chicago Press, 1984.

Kenyon, Kathleen M. *The Bible and Recent Archaeology*, rev. ed., ed. P. R. S. Moorey. Atlanta: John Knox Press, 1987.

Kitchen, K. A. *Pharaoh Triumphant: The Life and Times of Ramses II.* London: Aris and Phillips, 1982.

Knapp, A. Bernard. *The History and Culture of Ancient Western Asia and Egypt.* Chicago: The Dorsey Press, 1988.

————. "Response: Independence, Imperialism, and the Egyptian Factor." *Bulletin of the American Schools of Oriental Research* 275 (1989): 64–68.

Leonard, Albert, Jr. "The Late Bronze Age." *Biblical Archaeologist* 52 (1989): 4–39.

Liebowitz, Harold. "Response: LB IIB Ivories and the Material Culture of the Late Bronze Age." *Bulletin of the American Schools of Oriental Research* 275 (1989): 63–64.

Moran, William L. *Les lettres d'El Amarna: Correspondance diplomatique du pharaon.* Paris: Les Editions du Cerf, 1987.

Na'aman, Nadav. "Habiru and Hebrews: The Transfer of a Social Term to the Literary Sphere." *Journal of Near Eastern Studies* 45 (1986): 271–88.

Newby, P. H. *Warrior Pharaohs: The Rise and Fall of the Egyptian Empire.* London: Faber & Faber, 1980.

O'Connor, David. "New Kingdom and Third Intermediate Period, 1552–664 B.C." In *Ancient Egypt: A Social History*, ed. B. G. Trigger, B. J. Kemp, D. O'Connor, and A. B. Lloyd. Cambridge: Cambridge University Press, 1983.

Oren, Eliezer. "Governor's Residencies in Canaan under the New Kingdom: A Case Study of Egyptian Administration." *Journal of the Society for the Study of Egyptian Antiquities* 14 (1984): 37–56.

Pritchard, James B., ed., *Ancient Near Eastern Texts Relating to the Old Testament*, 3d ed. Princeton: Princeton University Press, 1969, 199–203, 234–63.

————, ed. *The Harper Atlas of the Bible.* New York: Harper & Row, 1987.

Rainey, Anson, ed. *Egypt, Israel, Sinai: Archaeological and Historical Relations in the Biblical Period.* Tel Aviv: Tel Aviv University, 1987.

Redford, Donald B. "The Ashkelon Relief at Karnak and the Israel Stela." *Israel Exploration Journal* 36(1986): 188–200.

————. "The Relations Between Egypt and Israel from El-Amarna to the Babylonian Conquest." In *Biblical Archaeology Today: Proceedings of the International Congress on Biblical Archaeology, Jerusalem, April 1984.* Jerusalem: Israel Exploration Society, 1985.

Singer, Itamar. "Merneptah's Campaign to Canaan and the Egyptian Occupation of the Southern Coastal Plain of Palestine in the

Ramesside Period." *Bulletin of the American Schools of Oriental Research* 269 (1988): 1–10.

Weinstein, James M. "The Egyptian Empire in Palestine: A Reassessment." *Bulletin of the American Schools of Oriental Research* 241 (1981): 1–28.

CHAPTER 3

Bienkowski, Piotr. *Jericho in the Late Bronze Age.* Warminster: Aris & Phillips, 1986.

Coote, Robert B., and Whitelam, Keith W. *The Emergence of Early Israel in Historical Perspective.* The Social World of Biblical Antiquity 5. Sheffield: Almond Press, 1987.

Gal, Zvi. "The Late Bronze Age in Galilee: A Reassessment." *Bulletin of the American Schools of Oriental Research* 272 (1988): 79–84.

———. "Kirbet Roš Zayit—Biblical Cabul." *Biblical Archaeologist* 53 (1990): 88–97.

Gonen, Rivka. "Urban Canaan in the Late Bronze Period." *Bulletin of the American Schools of Oriental Research* 253 (1984): 61–73.

Marfoe, Leon. "The Integrative Transformation: Patterns of Sociopolitical Organization in Southern Syria." *Bulletin of the American Schools of Oriental Research* 234 (1979): 1–42, 84.

Sauer, James A. "Transjordan in the Bronze and Iron Ages: A Critique of Glueck's Synthesis." *Bulletin of the American Schools of Oriental Research* 263 (1986): 1–26.

Wood, Bryant G. "Did the Israelites Conquer Jericho? A New Look at the Archaeological Evidence." *Biblical Archaeology Review* 16, no. 2 (March/April 1990): 44–58.

CHAPTER 4

Abu-Husayn, Abdul-Rahim. *Provincial Leaderships in Syria 1575–1650.* Syracuse, N.Y.: Syracuse University Press, 1986.

Abu-Lughod, Lila. *Veiled Sentiments: Honor and Poetry in a Bedouin Society.* Berkeley: University of California Press, 1986.

Ahlström, Gösta W. *Who Were the Israelites?* Winona Lake, Ind.: Eisenbrauns, 1986.

Bates, Daniel G., and Rassam, Amal. *Peoples and Cultures of the Middle East.* Englewood Cliffs, N.J.: Prentice-Hall, 1983.

Betts, Alison. "The Solubba: Nonpastoral Nomads in Arabia." *Bulletin of the American Schools of Oriental Research* 274 (1989): 61–69.

Coote, Robert B. "The Meaning of the Name Israel." *Harvard Theological Review* 65 (1972): 137–42.

Eickelman, Dale F. *The Middle East: An Anthropological Approach.* Englewood Cliffs, N.J.: Prentice-Hall, 1981.

Finkelstein, Israel. *The Archaeology of the Israelite Settlement*. Jerusalem: Israel Exploration Society, 1988.

Freedman, David Noel, and Graf, David Frank, eds., *Palestine in Transition: The Emergence of Ancient Israel*. The Social World of Biblical Antiquity 2. Sheffield: Almond Press, 1983.

Gottwald, Norman K. "The Israelite Settlement as a Social Revolutionary Movement." In *Biblical Archaeology Today: Proceedings of the International Congress on Biblical Archaeology, Jerusalem, April 1984*. Jerusalem: Israel Exploration Society, 1985.

Kamp, Kathryn A., and Yoffee, Norman. "Ethnicity in Ancient Western Asia During the Early Second Millennium B.C.: Archaeological Assessments and Ethnoarchaeological Prospectives." *Bulletin of the American Schools of Oriental Research* 237 (1980): 85–104.

Kelly, Raymond C. *The Nuer Conquest: The Structure and Development of an Expansionist System*. Ann Arbor: University of Michigan Press, 1985.

Knauf, Ernst Axel. *Ismael: Untersuchungen zur Geschichte Palästinas und Nordarabiens im 1. Jahrtausend v. Chr.* Wiesbaden: Otto Harrassowitz, 1985.

———. *Midian: Untersuchungen zur Geschichte Palästinas und Nordarabiens am Ende des 2. Jahrtausends v. Chr.* Wiesbaden: Otto Harrassowitz, 1988.

Kochavi, Moshe. "The Israelite Settlement in Canaan in the Light of Archaeological Surveys." In *Biblical Archaeology Today: Proceedings of the International Congress on Biblical Archaeology, Jerusalem, April 1984*. Jerusalem: Israel Exploration Society, 1985.

Lemche, Niels Peter. *Early Israel: Anthropological and Historical Studies on the Israelite Society before the Monarchy*. Leiden: E. J. Brill, 1985.

Martin, James D. "Israel as a Tribal Society." In *The World of Ancient Israel: Sociological, Anthropological and Political Perspectives*. Cambridge: Cambridge University Press, 1989.

Mayerson, Philip. "Saracens and Romans: Micro-Macro Relationships." *Bulletin of the American Schools of Oriental Research* 274 (1989): 71–79.

Mazar, Amihai. "The Israelite Settlement in Canaan in the Light of Archaeological Excavation." In *Biblical Archaeology Today: Proceedings of the International Congress on Biblical Archaeology, Jerusalem, April 1984*. Jerusalem: Israel Exploration Society, 1985.

Mazar, Benjamin, ed. *The World History of the Jewish People Vol. 2: Patriarchs*. Tel Aviv: Massada, 1970.

———, ed. *The World History of the Jewish People Vol. 3: Judges*. Tel Aviv: Massada, 1971.

Meeker, Michael E. *Literature and Violence in North Arabia*. Cambridge: Cambridge University Press, 1979.

Mendenhall, George E. *The Tenth Generation*. Baltimore: Johns Hopkins University Press, 1973.

Miller, J. Maxwell. "Old Testament History and Archaeology." *Biblical Archaeologist* 50 (1987): 55–63.

Redford, Donald B. "The Ashkelon Relief at Karnak and the Israel Stela." *Israel Exploration Journal* 36 (1986): 188–200.

Rosen, Steven A. "Finding Evidence of Ancient Nomads." *Biblical Archaeology Review* 14, no. 5 (September/October 1988): 46–53.

Rowton, Michael B. "Autonomy and Nomadism in Western Asia." *Orientalia* 42 (1973): 247–58.

———. "Urban Autonomy in a Nomadic Environment." *Journal of Near Eastern Studies* 32 (1973): 201–15.

———. "Dimorphic Structure and the Tribal Elite." *Al-Bahit: Festschrift Joseph Henninger, Studia Instituti Anthropos* 28 (1976): 219–57.

———. "Dimorphic Structure and the Parasocial Element." *Journal of Near Eastern Studies* 36 (1977): 181–98.

Sharon, Moshe. "The Political Role of the Bedouins in Palestine in the Sixteenth and Seventeenth Centuries." In *Studies on Palestine During the Ottoman Period*, ed. M. Ma'oz. Jerusalem: Magnes Press, 1975.

Shepherd, Naomi. "Feudal Palestine: Akil Aga." In *The Zealous Intruders: The Western Rediscovery of Palestine*. San Francisco: Harper & Row, 1987.

Stager, Lawrence E. "Merneptah, Israel and Sea Peoples: New Light on an Old Relief." *Eretz Israel* 18 (1985): 56*–64*.

Yurco, Frank J. "3,200-Year-Old Picture of Israelites Found in Egypt." *Biblical Archaeology Review* 16, no. 5 (September/October 1990): 20–38.

Zenner, Walter P. "Aqiili Agha: The Strongman in the Ethnic Relations of the Ottoman Galilee." *Comparative Studies in Society and History* 14 (1972): 169–88.

CHAPTER 5

Artzy, Michal. "On Boats and Sea Peoples." *Bulletin of the American Schools of Oriental Research* 266 (1987): 75–84.

Barag, Dan. "Survey of Pottery Recovered from the Sea off the Coast of Israel." *Israel Exploration Journal* 13 (1963): 13–19, plate v.

Brug, J. F. *A Literary and Archaeological Study of the Philistines.* B.A.R. International Series 265. Oxford: B.A.R., 1985.

Dothan, Moshe. "Ashdod at the End of the Late Bronze Age and the Beginning of the Iron Age." In *Symposia Celebrating the Seventy-Fifth Anniversary of the Founding of the American Schools of Oriental Research (1900–1975)*, ed. Frank Moore Cross. Cambridge: American Schools of Oriental Research, 1979.

Dothan, Trude. "The Philistines Reconsidered." In *Biblical Archaeology Today: Proceedings of the International Congress on Biblical Archaeology, Jerusalem, April 1984.* Jerusalem: Israel Exploration Society, 1985.

———. "Ekron of the Philistines, Part I: Where They Came From, How They Settled Down and the Place They Worshiped In." *Biblical Archaeology Review* 16, no. 1 (January/February 1990): 26–36.

———, and Gitin, Seymour. "Ekron of the Philistines: How They Lived, Worked and Worshiped for Five Hundred Years." *Biblical Archaeology Review* 16, no. 1 (January/February 1990): 20–25.

Gitin, Seymour, and Dothan, Trude. "The Rise and Fall of Ekron of the Philistines: Recent Excavations at an Urban Border Site." *Biblical Archaeologist* 50 (1987): 197–222.

Karageorghis, Vassos. "Exploring Philistine Origins on the Island of Cyprus." *Biblical Archaeology Review* 10, no. 2 (March/April 1984): 16–28.

Lattimore, Richmond. *The Odyssey of Homer.* New York: Harper & Row, 1965.

Mazar, Amihai. "The Emergence of the Philistine Material Culture." *Israel Exploration Journal* 35 (1985): 95–107.

Muhly, James D. "How Iron Technology Changed the Ancient World and Gave the Philistines a Military Edge." *Biblical Archaeology Review* 6, no. 6 (November/December 1982): 40–54.

Raban, Avner. "The Harbor of the Sea Peoples at Dor." *Biblical Archaeologist* 50 (1987): 118–26.

Sandars, Nancy K. *The Sea Peoples: Warriors of the Ancient Mediterranean*, rev. ed. London: Thames and Hudson, 1985.

Strange, John. "The Transition from the Bronze Age to the Iron Age in the Eastern Mediterranean and the Emergence of the Israelite State." *Scandinavian Journal of the Old Testament* 1 (1987): 1–19.

Tadmor, Hayim. "The Decline of Empires in Western Asia ca. 1200 B.C.E." In *Symposia Celebrating the Seventy-Fifth Anniversary of the Founding of the American Schools of Oriental Research*, ed. Frank Moore Cross. Cambridge: ASOR, 1979.

Waldbaum, Jane C. *From Bronze to Iron: The Transition from the Bronze Age to the Iron Age in the Eastern Mediterranean.* Göteburg: Paul Aströms Förlag, 1978.

Wood, Michael. *In Search of the Trojan War.* New York: Facts on File, 1985.

Yoffee, Norman, and Cowgill, George L., eds. *The Collapse of Ancient States and Civilizations.* Tucson: University of Arizona Press, 1988.

CHAPTER 6

Boling, Robert G., and Campbell, Edward F., Jr. "Jeroboam and Rehoboam at Shechem." In *Archaeology and Biblical Interpretation: Essays in Memory of D. Glenn Rose*, ed. Leo G. Perdue, Lawrence E. Toombs, and Gary L. Johnson. Atlanta: John Knox Press, 1987.

Callaway, Joseph A. "A Visit with Ahilud." *Biblical Archaeology Review* 9, no. 5 (September/October 1983): 42–53.

Coote, Robert B. "Settlement Change in Early Iron Age Palestine" (with response by David C. Hopkins). In *Early Israelite Agriculture: Reviews of David C. Hopkins' Book The Highlands of Canaan*, ed. Oystein Sakala La Bianca and David C. Hopkins *Occasional Papers of the Institute of Archaeology, Andrews University*, 1 (Berrien Springs, Mich.: Andrews University Press, 1988) 17–27.

————, and Whitelam, Keith W. "The Emergence of Israel: Social Transformation and State Formation Following the Decline in LBA Trade." *Semeia* 37 (1986): 107–47.

Currid, John D., and Gregg, Jeffrey L. "Why Did the Early Israelites Dig All Those Pits?" *Biblical Archaeology Review* 14, no. 5 (September/October 1988): 54–57.

————, and Navon, Avi. "Iron Age Pits and the Lahav (Tell Halif) Grain Storage Project." *Bulletin of the American Schools of Oriental Research* 273 (1989): 67–78.

Dever, William G. "The Contribution of Archaeology to the Study of Canaanite and Early Israelite Religion." In *Ancient Israelite Religion: Essays in Honor of Frank Moore Cross*, ed. Patrick D. Miller, Jr., et al. Philadelphia: Fortress Press, 1987.

————. *Recent Archaeological Discoveries and Biblical Research*. Seattle: University of Washington Press, 1990.

————, ed. [Papers from joint SBL/ASOR session on early Israel, Boston, Nov. 1987: forthcoming].

Edens, Christopher. Review of *The Emergence of Early Israel in Historical Perspective* by R. Coote and K. Whitelam; and of *The Archaeology of the Israelite Settlement* by I. Finkelstein. In *American Journal of Archaeology* 93(1989): 289–92.

Esse, Douglas L. Review of *The Archaeology of the Israelite Settlement* by I. Finkelstein. In *Biblical Archaeology Review* 14, no. 5 (September/October 1988): 6–12.

Finkelstein, Israel. "Arabian Trade and Socio-Political Conditions in the Negev in the Twelfth-Eleventh Centuries B.C.E." *Journal of Near Eastern Studies* 47 (1988): 241–52.

————. *The Archaeology of the Israelite Settlement*. Jerusalem: Israel Exploration Society, 1988.

————. "Searching for Israelite Origins." *Biblical Archaeology Review* 14, no. 5 (September/October 1988): 34–45.

Frick, Frank S. "Ecology, Agriculture and Patterns of Settlement." In *The World of Ancient Israel: Sociological, Anthropological and Political Perspectives,* ed. R. E. Clements. Cambridge: Cambridge University Press, 1989.

——. *The Formation of the State in Ancient Israel,* The Social World of Biblical Antiquity Series 4. Sheffield: Almond Press, 1985.

——. "Israelite State Formation in Iron I." In *Archaeology and Biblical Interpretation: Essays in Memory of D. Glenn Rose,* ed. Leo G. Perdue, Lawrence E. Toombs, and Gary L. Johnson. Atlanta: John Knox Press, 1987.

Fritz, Volkmar. "Conquest or Settlement? The Early Iron Age in Palestine." *Biblical Archaeologist* 50 (1987): 84–100.

Greenberg, Raphael. "New Light on the Early Iron Age at Tell Beit Mirsim." *Bulletin of the American Schools of Oriental Research* 265 (1987): 55–80.

Hesse, Brian. "Animal Use at Tel Miqne-Ekron in the Bronze Age and Iron Age." *Bulletin of the American Schools of Oriental Research* 264 (1986): 17–27.

Hopkins, David C. *The Highlands of Canaan.* Decatur and Sheffield: Almond Press, 1985.

——. "Life on the Land: The Subsistence Struggles of Early Israel." *Biblical Archaeologist* 50 (1987): 178–91.

Knauf, Ernst Axel. *Midian: Untersuchungen zur Geschichte Palästinas und Nordarabiens am Ende des 2. Jahrtausends v. Chr.* Wiesbaden: Harrassowitz, 1988.

Kochavi, Moshe. "The Israelite Settlement in Canaan in the Light of Archaeological Surveys." In *Biblical Archaeology Today: Proceedings of the International Congress on Biblical Archaeology, Jerusalem, April 1984.* Jerusalem: Israel Exploration Society, 1985.

London, Gloria. "A Comparison of Two Contemporaneous Lifestyles of the Late Second Millennium B.C." *Bulletin of the American Schools of Oriental Research* 273 (1989): 37–55.

Loretz, Oswald. *Habiru-Hebräer: Eine sozio-linguistische Studie über die Herkunft des Gentiliziums ᶜibri vom Appellativum habiru.* Berlin: Walter de Gruyter, 1984.

Mazar, Amihai. "Bronze Bull Found in Israelite 'High Place' from the Time of the Judges." *Biblical Archaeology Review* 9, no. 5 (September/October 1983): 34–40.

——. "The 'Bull Site'—An Iron Age I Open Cult Place." *Bulletin of the American Schools of Oriental Research* 247 (1982): 27–42.

——. "The Israelite Settlement in Canaan in the Light of Archaeological Excavations." In *Biblical Archaeology Today: Proceedings of the International Congress on Biblical Archaeology, Jerusalem, April 1984.* Jerusalem: Israel Exploration Society, 1985.

Meyers, Carol. "Of Seasons and Soldiers: A Topographical Appraisal of the Premonarchic Tribes of Galilee." *Bulletin of the American Schools of Oriental Research* 252 (1983): 47–59.

Miller, J. Maxwell, and Hayes, John H. *A History of Ancient Israel and Judah*. Philadelphia: Westminster Press, 1986.

Otto, Eckart. "Israels Wurzeln in Kanaan: Auf dem Weg zu einer neuen Kultur- und Sozialgeschichte des antiken Israels." *Theologische Revue* 85, no. 1 (1989): 3–10.

Rainey, Anson F. "Biblical Archaeology Yesterday (and Today)." *Bulletin of the American Schools of Oriental Research* 273 (1989): 87–96.

Shiloh, Yigal. "The Casemate Wall, the Four Room House, and Early Planning in the Israelite City." *Bulletin of the American Schools of Oriental Research* 268 (1987): 3–15.

Stager, Lawrence E. "The Archaeology of the Family in Ancient Israel." *Bulletin of the American Schools of Oriental Research* 260 (1985): 1–35.

———. "The Song of Deborah—Why Some Tribes Answered the Call and Others Did Not." *Biblical Archaeology Review* 15, no. 1 (January/February 1989): 50–64.

Zertal, Adam. "How Can Kempinski Be So Wrong?" *Biblical Archaeology Review* 12, no. 1 (January/February 1986): 43, 49-53.

CHAPTER 7

Bynum, David E. "Samson as a Biblical *phēr oreskǭos*." In Susan Niditch, ed., *Text and Tradition: The Hebrew Bible and Folklore*, Semeia Studies. Forthcoming.

Chaney, Marvin L. "Joshua." In *The Books of the Bible*, vol. 1. New York: Scribner's, 1989.

Coote, Robert B. *The Elohist: In Defense of Revolution*. Minneapolis: Fortress Press, forthcoming.

———, and Ord, David R. *The Bible's First History*. Philadelphia: Fortress Press, 1989.

Finkelstein, Israel. "The Emergence of the Monarchy in Israel: The Environmental and Socio-Economic Aspects." *Journal for the Study of the Old Testament* 44 (1989): 43–74.

Flanagan, James W. "Chiefs in Israel." *Journal for the Study of the Old Testament* 20 (1981): 47–73.

———. *David's Social Drama: A Hologram of Israel's Early Age*, The Social World of Biblical Antiquity 7. Sheffield: Sheffield Academic Press, 1989.

Frick, Frank S. "Israelite State Formation in Iron I." In *Archaeology and Biblical Interpretation: Essays in Memory of D. Glenn Rose*, ed. Leo G. Perdue, Lawrence E. Toombs, and Gary L. Johnson. Atlanta: John Knox Press, 1987.

Halpern, Baruch. *The First Historians: The Hebrew Bible and History*. San Francisco: Harper & Row, 1988.

Haver, Christian E., Jr. "David and the Levites." *Journal for the Study of the Old Testament* 23 (1982): 33–54.

Levenson, Jon D., and Halpern, Baruch. "The Political Import of David's Marriages." *Journal of Biblical Literature* 99 (1980): 507–18.

McCarter, P. Kyle, Jr. "The Historical Abraham." *Interpretation* 42 (1988): 341–52.

———. "The Historical David." *Interpretation* 40 (1986): 117–29.

———. "The Patriarchal Age: Abraham, Isaac and Jacob." In *Ancient Israel: A Short History from Abraham to the Roman Destruction of the Temple*, ed. Hershel Shanks. Washington, D.C.: Biblical Archaeology Society; Englewood Cliffs, N.J.: Prentice-Hall, 1988.

Miller, J. Maxwell, and Hayes, John H. *A History of Ancient Israel and Judah*. Philadelphia: Westminster Press, 1986.

Olyan, Saul. "Zadok's Origins and the Tribal Politics of David." *Journal of Biblical Literature* 101 (1982): 177–93.

Stager, Lawrence E. "The Song of Deborah—Why Some Tribes Answered the Call and Others Did Not." *Biblical Archaeology Review* 15, no. 1 (January/February 1989): 50–64.

Whitlam, Keith W. "The Defense of David." *Journal for the Study of the Old Testament* 29 (1984): 61–87.

———. "The Symbols of Power: Aspects of Royal Propaganda in the United Monarchy." *Biblical Archaeologist* 49 (1986): 166–73.

CHAPTER 8

Coogan, Michael David. "Canaanite Origins and Lineage: Reflections on the Religion of Ancient Israel." In *Ancient Israelite Religion: Essays in Honor of Frank Moore Cross*, ed. Patrick D. Miller, Jr., et al. Philadelphia: Fortress Press, 1987.

Coote, Robert B., and Coote, Mary P. *Power, Politics, and the Making of the Bible*. Minneapolis: Fortress Press, 1990.

Garbini, Giovanni. *History and Ideology in Ancient Israel*. New York: Crossroad, 1988.

Index